Library Communication.

THE LANGUAGE OF LEADERSHIP

edited by

Donald E. Riggs

American Library Association

CHICAGO AND LONDON 1991

Cover and text designed by Harriett Banner

Composed by Digital Graphics, Inc. in Sabon and Trump Medieval using TEX. Reproduction copy set on a Varityper 4300P imagesetter

Printed on 50-pound Glatfelter, a pH-neutral stock, and bound in 10-point C1S Braun-Brumfield, Inc.

The paper used in this publication meets the minimum requirements of American National Standard for Information Sciences—Permanence of Paper for Printed Library Materials, ANSI Z39.48-1984. ∞

Library of Congress Cataloging-in-Publication Data
Library communication : the language of leadership / edited by Donald
  E. Riggs.
    p.   cm.
  Includes bibliographical references.
  ISBN 0-8389-0581-1
    1. Communication in library administration. 2. Communication in
  library science. I. Riggs, Donald E.
  Z678.L46   1992
  025.1–dc20   91-34565

Printed in the United States of America.

95 94 93 92 91   5 4 3 2 1

Contents

iii

383509

Foreword

In these times, with the amount of information growing exponentially and with so many Americans working in the information field, effective communication in the library profession is essential. Librarians have worthy causes to sell and varied groups to educate and to motivate. Some of these people work in libraries and some work on behalf of libraries—legislators, administrators, other library supporters, and users.

At present, developing people skills is a major focus of library continuing education. Key among these skills is the ability to communicate—to observe, to listen, to speak, and, perhaps most important, to write. Valuable as these talents are to all librarians, they are *essential* to library leaders, who must articulate visions, communicate purposes, and motivate others to follow, in part by providing recognition and appreciation. It is this symbiotic relationship between leadership and communication about which the Library Administration and Management Association (LAMA) solicited comment in these essays on "The Language of Leadership," one of the two themes of my presidency.

Writing itself is, of course, an important instructional activity, but it is only one part of the job. Another is packaging, the "look" of a book, an article, a brochure, or any other document. The medium is part of the message. Like punishment, the style of communicating should fit its cause. Surely not every communique from a library director's office need be fully packed with staid, bureaucratic prose.

True leaders command attention when they speak or write, but not just because of their positions. They spend time and energy communicating with many different kinds of people, a task they accomplish best when they listen first so that they know what kind of message will achieve their purposes.

As I read a recent book—*Secrets of Effective Leadership* by F. A. Manske, senior vice president of Federal Express—I was struck by the amount of time that the author recommends leaders spend communicating with *all* levels of employees, not just those in the reporting chain. I was also struck by his recommendations that leaders share information openly and willingly; that they be lifelong learners; that they read in a broad range of fields, including fiction; and that they find the energy to stay in touch with the "outside world," participating in their communities and knowing well the contexts in which their leadership lives.

Generating the raw material for this book—that is, the papers on the title topic—was one of the most important activities LAMA undertook during my term as its president. I welcome this opportunity to thank all of the authors.

Earlier, Louis I. Middleman, who had moderated the 1988 Midwinter LAMA planning session, inferred LAMA's corporate culture from our written record—that is, from statements of goals and objectives, reports, our magazine, and other publications—and helped us see that we weren't understanding or communicating our *own* case very well. We knew we were busy; after his session we had a better idea about what we were busy *about*, and we saw the need for change. Finally, former Deputy Librarian of Congress William J. Welsh, our dinner speaker in New Orleans, showed us how to communicate our agenda better as we become more active agents in the democratic process.

When I sought help in reading the papers that had been submitted, I asked, "Does anyone see a book here?" (I did not ask, "Does anyone *else* see a book here?"). By return mail I had from Don Riggs a fully developed proposal for this book. Now *that* is communication of the finest sort—intelligent and thoughtful, substantive, responsive, immediate, and exciting—and it is also the behavior of a leader, one to whom I and the Library Administration and Management Association are most grateful.

ANN HEIDBREDER EASTMAN

Introduction

Communication has looked so large and has become so vital as a part of leadership that it is indeed difficult to ascertain where one commences and the other intermeshes.

Harold Zelko and Frank E. X. Dance

Leadership is a topic that has gotten much coverage recently in books and journals; however, for some unexplainable reason there is a noticeable shortage of works on leadership in librarianship: Fewer than a half dozen books are devoted to the subject; several books and journal articles are available on improving communication in libraries. Nevertheless, little information, if any, exists on the role of communication in library leadership.

An all-encompassing definition of communication is that it is any transfer of meaning from one person to another. One of the least noticeable influences on our behavior is the language we use. Sharing a language with other persons provides the subtlest and most powerful of all tools for controlling the behavior of other persons for the benefit of an organization. Meanings of words change roughly as fast as the enacted environment changes, and the rate of language renewal will need to keep pace if leadership effectiveness is to be sustained. What is communicated in a communication is not words, but meanings. The dimensions of communication include intentional-unintentional, verbal-nonverbal, oral-written, formal-informal, and internal-external. Communication is a complex process that is dynamic in nature (i.e., always changing, never static). Communication is going on at all times.

Daniel Katz and Robert I. Kahn point out that communication from leader to follower is basically of five types (all covered in this book):

1. Specific task directives: *Job instructions.*
2. Information designed to produce understanding of the task and its relationship to other organizational tasks: *Job rationale.*
3. Information about organizational *procedures* and *practices.*
4. *Feedback* to the subordinate about his or her performance.
5. Information of an ideological character to inculcate a sense of mission: *Indoctrination of goals.*[1]

Motivation, persuasion, influence, or any other leadership activity that might seek to elicit greater dedication or effort is almost totally dependent on the flow of communication. The job of the leader is, ultimately, communication, regardless of how varied or specialized the activity of the moment. Libraries are human organizations that are organized to gain specified goals. Attainment of these goals is far more dependent upon leadership and communication than we would normally imagine. Leaders lead by pulling (persuading) rather than by pushing, by inspiring rather than by ordering, and by empowering the library staff to use their own initiative and experiences rather than by denying or constraining their experiences and actions. Libraries are undergoing rapid changes (e.g., implementation of new technology) and experiencing some confusion about their future. External forces are playing a greater role in determining the library of tomorrow. It is as if librarianship, to paraphrase Teilhard de Chardin, is falling out of control of its destiny. Perhaps a new Homer or Herodotus will be able to show us its patterns and designs, its coherences and contours. What we hear and discern now is not one voice or signal but a confusing mishmash of chords. All we know for sure is that we cannot wait a generation for the historian to tell us what happened; we must try to make sense out of the jumble of voices now.[2]

Many libraries are well managed but poorly led. They may excel in the ability to handle daily routine, and yet they may never ask whether the routine should be done at all. To lead, the dictionary informs us, is to go in advance of, to show the way, to influence or induce, to guide in direction, course, action, or opinion. We need leaders at every level throughout the library; department heads in a library construct should function as leaders. Warren G. Bennis and Burt Nanus describe the difference between leadership and management as follows:

The distinction between management and leadership is crucial. Managers are people who do things right and leaders are people who do the right thing. The difference may be summarized as activities of vision and judgment—*effectiveness* versus activities of mastering routines—*efficiency*.[3]

Leadership implies that the holder is visionary, to paraphrase Shelley, to see the present in the past and the future in the present. Developing a vision for the library is not enough. Library leaders must know how to harness the vision and bring it to fruition. The vision must be credible, realistic, and supported by a consensus within the library. Moreover, the library leadership must communicate effectively how the vision will be achieved. Communication is the way library leaders can bridge the gaps, stay in touch, build trust, monitor performance, and attain the concerted vision. The best communication process forces one to listen. Without good listening, the transfer of meaning is impossible. Wise leaders are continually finding ways to say to their constituents, "I hear you." Simplicity and clarity in communication are very important. The library leader's behavior is another important form of communication: Communication through behavior happens all the time in libraries. The formulation and articulation of values create the library's life blood. Without effective communication, actively practiced, those values will disappear in a sea of trivial memos and impertinent reports. There may be no single thing more important for library leaders in their efforts to achieve meaningful work and fulfilling relationships than to learn and practice the art of communication.[4] The real power of Martin Luther King, Jr. was not only that he had a dream, but that he could communicate it. This dual capacity to make sense of things and to put them into meaningful language gives the leader enormous leverage.

The sixteen essays included in this volume focus on practical and theoretical aspects of the importance of communication in leadership and describe various ways of improving library leadership via effective communication. The contributors include practicing librarians (from various types of libraries) and educators. One thread that runs through the articles is that effective two-way communication is essential to proper functioning of the leader-follower relationship. Leaders, to be effective, must pick up and comprehend signals coming to them from followers. Communication is paramount in the leader's success in resolving conflicts and in coalition building. The contributing authors repeatedly emphasize that only through effective communication can the library leader establish direction, formulate action strategies, and help create the future. Communication enables library leaders to project a vision and to persuade their colleagues that the vision is worthy of transformation into reality.

I, like Ann Eastman, am grateful to the contributors for providing these essays on a timely topic. We all tend to agree that communication is not only the most important leadership tool, but that leadership is, in essence, communication.

Edna St. Vincent Millay may just as well have been thinking about the magnitude of communication and information and their importance to leadership when she wrote:

> Upon this gifted age, in its dark hour,
> Rains from the sky a meteoric shower
> Of facts . . . they lie unquestioned, uncombined.
> Wisdom enough to leech us or our ill
> Is daily spun; but there exists no loom
> To weave into fabric . . .

DONALD E. RIGGS

References

1. Daniel Katz and Robert I. Kahn, *The Social Psychology of Organizations* (New York: Wiley, 1966), 302.
2. Warren G. Bennis, "Where Have All the Leaders Gone?" *Technology Review* 2 (March–April 1977): 38.
3. Warren G. Bennis and Burt Nanus, *Leaders: The Strategies for Taking Charge* (New York: Harper & Row, 1985), 21.
4. Max De Pree, *Leadership Is an Art* (East Lansing: Michigan State University, 1987), 102.

Part One

The Knitting Together of Communication and Leadership

God gave us two ears and only one mouth. In view of the way we use these, it is probably a very good thing that this is not reversed.

Cicero

Good communication, like clean air, is usually taken for granted until its absence begins to make life unpleasant. Of course, we can always count on some sage diagnostician to step forward and explain what went wrong. The wise one carefully surveys the wreckage of an enterprise and delivers the verdict: "What we have here is a problem in communication." Whether one knows all the answers or not, it is seldom wrong to suggest that communication breakdown is the cause of failure. Wherever you go, the same elementary failure to make the message clear inevitably foils the best laid plans.

In his management classic, *The Functions of the Executive*, Chester I. Barnard says, "A business organization consists of persons who are both able to communicate with one another, willing to serve, and united to accomplish a common purpose or goal." [1] Thus it would appear that communication is a key to leadership effectiveness. It is the library leader's responsibility to take the initiative in the communication process, to set the communication agenda, oral and written, as well as formal and informal. Leaders in libraries need to communicate policies, instructions, objectives, and goals so that all library employees will understand and accept them. There is no better leadership magic to hold and control peo-

1

ple than understanding. The final test of communication is whether it produces the desired results quickly and correctly.

Communication and leadership must function like "hand in glove." They must be knitted together in a manner that allows messages to be conveyed effectively throughout the library. Leaders, through communication, should develop a relationship with their library constituents that is mutually nourishing and strengthening. This relationship is not bland, nor is it without tension and conflict. The reconciling of divergent purposes in the library is one of the classic tasks of any leader. We expect our library leaders to be sensitive to and serve the basic needs of their followers. Faith in their constituents and a caring concern for them are other normal expectations of library leaders.

Achieving the library's goals requires nothing short of an organization that promotes teamwork throughout its construct. The team relationship will undoubtedly depend on inter- or intradepartmental communication. The messages, spoken and written, must be clear and concise. Leaders have little time to filter through long memos looking for the "gist" of them. In order to achieve the aspirations of the library, leadership will have to be persuasive and make the best use of the unique human potential on the team.

The interactions between leaders and followers in a library are not unlike interactions in other organizations. Mutual goals and shared values are common elements in the leader-follower environment. Almost any well-run library is likely to have a set of rules—sometimes they are called policies, procedures, or guidelines—designed not to restrict creativity but to assist members in the accomplishment of library goals. Libraries, like people, have personalities. To survive, libraries require a reasonable amount of predictability and order. The larger the library, the greater the formality in its structure. Formal structures necessitate a higher level of sophistication in communication as the rules must be continually aligned with goals and objectives.

As library leaders develop better communication mechanisms they should be seeking ways to enhance creativity. Librarians in a well-communicated environment should be inspired to see useful relationships among dissimilar things in their working environment. Looking for useful relationships among seemingly unrelated library activities will enable the library staff to develop ideas and solutions to problems that they previously felt incapable of handling. The inquisitive and innovative librarian is rare. Leadership, through communication, needs to set the stage for the library staff to make new applications of older concepts, and to be receptive and open-minded to new ideas.

The interdependence between communication and leadership requires special emphasis. Libraries are undergoing many changes and must have forward-thinking, dynamic leadership. Leadership effectiveness is highly dependent on communication effectiveness. This symbiotic relationship, if coordinated properly, will pay many dividends to library employees and the users they serve.

Reference

1. Chester I. Barnard, *The Functions of the Executive* (Cambridge, Mass.: Harvard University Press, 1938), 226.

1

Language, Leadership, and Librarians

H. Rebecca Kroll

The theme "The Language of Leadership" is an attention-catching, alliterative phrase that identifies a topic of critical importance, not just in libraries, but in organizations of all kinds. A great deal of attention recently has been focused on leadership in American corporations and in the political arena. There is a justifiable need to identify leadership qualities in our potential presidents. Anything that leads to critical thinking on the topic of leadership, whether on a national, organizational, or small group level, is probably very healthy. This chapter is concerned not with the outward trappings of leadership as displayed through language, but with the use of language as a tool to gain a position of leadership, to improve the caliber of leadership, or to expand the territory of leadership in any situation—and in libraries in particular.

The purpose of all language is communication. In order to understand how to use the language of leadership most effectively, it is necessary to understand the communication process, a combination of art and science that in some circles has been elevated to the status of "communication engineering." This chapter will begin with a brief analysis of the process of communication (spoken, written, and nonverbal), with an emphasis on nonverbal forms, some of which are not normally considered ways of communicating, but which can have an enormous impact on a target audience. After reviewing the communication aspect, this chapter will address the leadership aspect, with an overview of the literature and a review of ways to approach the analysis of leadership. The third section will put the two concepts together and suggest some real-world applications for the theory that has been presented.

Language and Beyond

This section deals with the communication process and with the type of information that is unwittingly conveyed, but not intended, during that process. To understand how this happens, it helps to remember the separate factors that make up an act of communication. In its most basic form, communication can be diagrammed as a message M which is transmitted from sender S to receiver R:

$$/S/ - (M) \longrightarrow /R/$$

This message may consist of words, spoken or written, of pictures in the form of drawings or photographs, of symbols, or of gestures. In order for communication to take place, R successfully receives M from S. In the simplest of all possible worlds, that would be all there was to it. In the pressure of daily life and work, it is easy to forget that successful communication is not as straightforward as our diagram.

If S is a real person, he or she carries at all times the combined riches and burdens of experience, learning, personality, and ethnic background, to name just a few of the factors that influence the content and transmission of the message S wishes to send. On the other end, R is similarly favored and burdened, so that with the best will in the world to be open and receptive, R may not, in fact, receive the message that S was trying to send. Furthermore, that good will is often partially lacking, since R may deliberately or unconsciously screen out some of the less welcome incoming information. Add to this confusion the truism that nothing happens in a vacuum:

$$/S/ - E - (M) - E \longrightarrow /R/$$

S and R are surrounded by their environment E, through which the message must pass from one to the other. The environment may act sometimes as a filter and sometimes as an amplifier so that the message may arrive distorted in any number of ways. Anyone who has played the children's party game where a sentence is whispered around the table and in the process is transformed into a set of words having no connection with the original sentence will agree that obfuscation occurs more readily than communication. What makes it all so difficult?

Let us start with the message itself, which possesses two attributes of immediate concern: form and content. The message content—the actual information to be transmitted—could in itself occupy an entire book. In fact, volumes have been written about speaking and writing clearly, targeting language to the intended audience, and using proven techniques for inducing feedback and assuring comprehension at the other end of the message chain. All of us who have worked a reference desk or supervised a single staff member are familiar with the pitfalls of trying to transmit a "simple, straightforward" message.

Less immediately obvious, but of equal importance, is the other message attribute: form. Consider the impact of hearing that a complaint has been received about your department, delivered three possible ways: (1) passed on informally during a chance encounter near the water fountain, (2) broached formally as a telephone request to attend a meeting about the problem, or (3) raised by memo from the office of the director. Depending on your own personality, your relationship with the upper administration, and the overall communication practices in your library, any one of these may be interpreted as a signal that a small matter has come up that can be routinely dealt with, or as a warning of impending disaster. What is your preferred style of communication? Do you switch from voice to paper as problems become more serious? Or do you deal with routine things by memo because there is no urgency, but pick up the phone, or hit the warpath in person as matters escalate? The form in which you send or receive the message can mean as much as the content of that message. There is no one "right" way to transmit information, but it is important that the sender and the receiver agree on what the form conveys.

The form of the message, while perhaps the easiest example to analyze, is just one example of nonverbal communication. For most of us, the most familiar nonverbal communication consists of gestures accompanying spoken words. One report claims that "no more than 35 percent of the social message in a conversation is spoken—the rest is nonverbal."[1] Research on nonverbal communication has been popularized by books such as Julius Fast's *Body Language*;[2] more scholarly works dissect nonverbal signs into performance codes, artifactual codes, mediational codes, and contextual codes. Performance codes include gestures, facial expressions, and sounds such as laughter or yawns. A speaker on a platform receives constant feedback of this kind from the audience; from the point of view of the platform, head nodding and note taking are good signs, while blank stares and watch checking are not! Artifactual codes most commonly include type of dress and use of cosmetics, but also include furnishings, art objects, and architecture. The "dress for success" school is based on this very real contribution of clothing to the overall message. Mediational codes come into play, as the name conveys, in various media: the cropping or enlarging of photographs and the choice of color or black-and-white are two examples. The same thought process should go into the selection of color and weight of paper for a résumé, or the choice of a formal, typed cover memo on letterhead versus a handwritten note clipped casually to the top of a document. A fourth group consists of contextual codes, where time and space are used to support communication. This cosmic-sounding manipulation may be as simple as the placement of an administrator's desk squarely facing the entrance of the office, or the scheduling of a staff meeting at 4:30 on Friday afternoon. Both convey something about the administrator's attitude to the job and the people.

While not all of these categories are applicable to all communication situations, most of them will be operative most of the time, which brings us to what I consider the ABC's of communication: *Attitudes, Behaviors,* and *Choices.* Each time sender *S* communicates something, *S* knowingly or unwittingly displays an attitude, commits a behavior, and makes choices about the subject being addressed or about the receiver of the message. Much has been written in library literature about nonverbal communication at the reference desk: the reference librarian who pores closely over a professional journal while working the desk, treats questions as untimely interruptions, and uses the reference desk chair as a throne from which to point patrons in the right direction is sending out a completely different message from that other stereotype who keeps a weather eye out for bewildered patrons, readily establishes eye contact reinforced with raised eyebrows or smiles, and leaps to a standing position when someone approaches the reference desk. Much less has been written about the impact of similar nonverbal messages transmitted by library administrators, who also go through the day displaying a constant stream of attitudes, behaviors, and choices. Some applications for these categories of nonverbal communication codes will be discussed in the final section of this chapter.

Leadership

There are two ways of looking at the concept of leadership in relation to libraries: leadership within the library as practiced by members of the library staff, and leadership by libraries and librarians in the world outside the library. Both are valid concepts, and both require well-honed communications skills.

First, however, a word about leadership. It is significant that we are focusing on "leadership" rather than on "management." Management and leadership are not interchangeable. Managers should be able to lead and leaders should be able to manage, but understanding the difference is critical to our success in the future. Management consists of determining measurable, realistic goals and objectives, setting up the operations to achieve those goals, and then assessing the results. Leadership consists of getting people together to define and successfully pursue the goals.

There are almost as many definitions of leadership as there are writers on the topic. James MacGregor Burns opens a text on leadership with the comment that "leadership is one of the most observed and least understood phenomena."[3] My favorite definition is an unidentified comment from the cover of Kenneth H. Blanchard's *Leadership and the One-Minute Manager*, "When the best leader's work is done, the people say 'we did it ourselves!' "[4]

While in many ways leadership is an art with which some people seem to be naturally endowed while others are not (a "leaders-are-born" approach), in other ways leadership ability consists of identifiable traits and skills that can be analyzed, defined, and learned (a "leaders-are-made" approach). Since leadership is such an amorphous concept—everyone "knows" what is meant by it, but no two people agree on its constituent parts—attempts have been made to segment leadership into a set of skills or a set of traits, in the hope of learning not only how it works, but how to predict who will be a successful leader and who will not.

Two major predictors of success that have been postulated to date are leadership traits and leadership behavior. The theory is that certain attributes or certain ways of behaving are more conducive to achieving and maintaining a successful leadership role than others. Typical traits for which almost all studies show positive correlation with successful leadership include high intelligence, initiative, willingness to assume responsibility, self-assurance, emotional stability, and a sense of humor.[5]

Leadership behavior refers more to a method or style of leadership. One method of analysis differentiates between task-oriented and people-oriented leadership styles. Another differentiates between "supportive" and "directive" behavior on the part of the leader: the directive leader issues orders or instructions; the supportive leader listens, facilitates and encourages followers to develop their own solutions. A leader may also use a blend of the two behaviors. More recently, the term "situational leadership" has come in vogue along with the view that, while there is no single "best" style of leadership, in any situation there will be a style that will be predictably better than others. Situational leadership focuses not only on the person in charge (frequently the sender of the message), but also on the subordinate (the receiver of the message) and on the environment of their interaction. Blanchard outlines four leadership styles: directing, coaching, supporting, and delegating.[6] He has established a matrix of supportive and directive behavior styles:

	Not Directive	Very Directive
Very Supportive	SUPPORTING	COACHING
Not Supportive	DELEGATING	DIRECTING

The essence of situational leadership is that all four styles are appropriate at certain times: A beginning librarian with little on the job training or experience may require "coaching," which the matrix shows to be very supportive and very directive. A committed librarian learning a new area of competency may require the "directing" approach, which teaches how to deal with the new area without having to motivate. These arbitrary categories, of course, need to be applied with common sense and a sense of humor. Remember the days when librarians with ten years' experience on the reference desk were learning on-line searching for the first time? The crux of situational leadership lies in examining all facets of the situation before selecting a particular style for a particular set of circumstances and in knowing when to adjust that style as either the circumstances or the people change.

How do traits and styles of leadership, and situational leadership in particular, relate to the communication theory reviewed in the earlier section? The ABC's—Attitudes, Behaviors, and Choices—apply to leadership as well as to communication. The classic "Theory X" and "Theory Y" schools of management (X—that workers are basically unwilling and need to be constantly prodded and threatened into productivity; Y—that workers are intrinsically interested in doing a good job and should be motivated and rewarded accordingly) are explanations of Attitude on the part of management toward workers and leaders to followers. The librarian who starts with the premise that cooperation and commitment do not come naturally will plan differently, behave differently, and certainly communicate differently than the librarian who firmly believes that one's people want to do the best possible job for the library and for themselves. Effective leadership serves as a linchpin when migrating employees from Theory X to Theory Y; this migration will require understanding, empathy, and sound communication.

Applications

How do we apply the theory outlined here in a real-world, functioning library situation? Most of us feel there is not enough time in the day to get the work done, let alone to review alphabetical communication theories before picking up the telephone or revving up the word processor. One place to start is by looking at what we are doing now and deciding in the context of communication and leadership what kind of work atmosphere we are fostering with present attitudes, behaviors, and choices. For example, the library can be viewed as a communication network with its information channels being analyzed. How does information travel inside the library? Is it "top-down," consisting of a series of directives from the library administration? Is there two-way communication, allowing reactions and feedback from staff during the planning process? Is it largely a "bottom-up" consultative process with staff heavily involved from the beginning? It also helps to look for communication barriers cutting down the information flow between the outside world and the library. Library staff need to be aware of what is happening on their campus, in their municipality, or in their company that may affect their work. Trustees, campus administrators, and corporate staff need to be aware of what goes on in the library in order to appreciate its potential. All of these represent communication channels where the language of leadership can be applied.

Beginning inside the library, we have already noted the difference in the image of the library fostered by two exaggerated stereotypes of reference librarian behavior at the desk—going from intimidating to accommodating. We all try, on our good days at least, to be as friendly and as helpful as possible when dealing with our patrons, but we should also examine our interactions with library colleagues. There are times when it seems impossible to accomplish any work because people are constantly "interrupting"—but people are what keeps the library going. The best budget and the best collection could not be used or useful without the people who provide the organization and access. Applying the language of leadership in the library means many things. It means applying the ABC's of communication in everyday dealings until it becomes second nature to use the right approach, the right tone, and the right words to fit the situation.

In planning, it means maintaining a visibly positive and constructive attitude toward patrons, staff, and problems. This in turn filters down throughout the organization, encouraging the whole staff of the department, the unit, or the branch to view it as a dynamic workplace where the emphasis is on accomplishments, not problems. It means deliberately selecting behaviors that put that department or library in the forefront of the action—experimenting, demonstrating, and acting rather than reacting—and doing this requires a lot of *planning* followed by a lot of *doing*. It means consciously choosing to move ahead rather than hold still, to constantly ask "why" and "why not," and to behave in such a way that the whole team feels comfortable doing the same thing.

In dealing with library staff, applying the language of leadership means adjusting interactive and management styles to maximize the potential of the particular people in the particular situation. It means making conscious choices that take into account the long-term effects of short-term actions. We all carry on our work, some of it routine, some of it challenging, although sometimes the challenge seems to be one of endurance rather than innovation. Communicating in the language of leadership means working to avoid frustrating interactions with colleagues over the routine tasks so that the information channels are cleared and ready for action when interesting assignments or intriguing possibilities appear.

The need for the language of leadership does not diminish outside the library—if anything, it is even stronger. Librarians need to convey to all of those who use and view the library that this is where information management takes place: we acquire it, we display it, and—perhaps most important of all—we can teach faculty, students, community patrons, and corporate clients how to do it for themselves. Libraries and librarians should be taking the lead in all forms of information management. They should look at the present trend toward greater end-user involvement not as a threat, but as an opportunity for even greater service to various clienteles.

Whether we are convincing the community of the need for a new approach to resource sharing, or involving the library staff in planning for direct linkage between client workstations and library services, we can—and should—be the ones in control, building a foundation for the information era to come.

References

1. Flora Davis, *Inside Intuition: What We Know about Non-Verbal Communication* (New York: McGraw-Hill, 1973), 25.
2. Julius Fast, *Body Language* (New York: M. Evans, 1970).
3. James MacGregor Burns, *Leadership* (New York: Harper & Row, 1978), 1.
4. Kenneth H. Blanchard, *Leadership and the One-Minute Manager:*

Increasing Effectiveness through Situational Leadership (New York: William Morrow, 1985).

5. Ralph Melvin Stogdill, *Stogdill's Handbook of Leadership: A Survey of Theory and Research*, an expanded edition by Bernard M. Bass (New York: Free Press, 1981), 9.

6. Blanchard, *Leadership*, 68.

2

Effective Communication: High-Level Management Receptive to Low-Level Management Ideas

JUNE D. CHRESSANTHIS AND KELLY JANOUSEK

The job advertisement reads:

> Anyname library: Librarian II. Required: ALA-MLS; strong interpersonal skills; willingness to develop and participate in existing services; can communicate effectively with all levels of clients. Preferred: Strong evidence of managerial skills and independent judgment.

This example of a generic job description found in today's professional literature is a common delineation of the type of leadership qualities the entry-level manager candidate is expected to have. Yet why do entrants feel their expected leadership qualities are seldom utilized? Are high-level managers afraid to use their potential ideas by incorporating their thoughts into daily policies and procedures? Does senior management fear a loss of power or control? Lower-level managers naturally perceive their supervisors as leadership mentors, yet many times established managers do not seem to exhibit basic qualities expected in the entrant.

Junior staff or low-level managers are those who are new to the library profession or new to the library organization. They usually have minimal supervisory duties. Basically, they are on the bottom rung of the management ladder.

Senior staff or high-level managers make final decisions. Depending upon the nature of given problems, decision makers may be library directors, area supervisors, or department heads. High-level managers have the knowledge and experience required to make necessary daily decisions. These positions carry with them a degree of power and respect. Donald E. Riggs stated:

> Power is not a process that necessarily has to hurt anybody, and it does not have to be hostile; it is simply the ability to make decisions, to take risks, to lead, and to get things done.[1]

Those who have power are in the position to be effective leaders. They should and can foster an atmosphere of receptiveness for innovations and positive attitudes by giving support to junior staff members' ideas, trusting in their professional abilities, encouraging them to strive for excellence, and keeping open communication lines. Of course not all ideas offered by junior staff members will be practical or even worthwhile, but their ideas need to be given a fair hearing by high-level management. Otherwise, how will low-level managers know the caliber of their concepts unless library leaders are listening and giving feedback?

The following scenarios describe communication patterns the low-level manager might use to transmit potential ideas or policies. Two characters, Jane and Dick, will be used to exemplify the scenarios. Jane and Dick are traditional, new academic library employees.

A new book title for acquisition must be submitted to Jane's supervisor, then to the head of reference, then to the associate director for public services, and finally to the library director. Jane wondered why two or three people had to approve the purchase of a $3.96 pamphlet on child abuse. Jane presented to her supervisor a written recommendation that in cases of normal book purchases, order requests should go to the head of reference. Only those of $150.00 or more should be perused by the associate director for public services. The library director really had no need to see each individual book acquisition. In this scenario, Jane adhered to the rules by submitting a written recommendation for a new policy to the hierarchy as described in her manual of procedures. A procedures manual offers the first authoritative contact a junior staff member has in communicating upward through the administrative structure, hence this is the most likely channel to be used by them.

Meanwhile, our other new employee, Dick, noticed that the microfilm reader-printer was usually out of order. He became upset as the situation continued even after he requested to have the equipment replaced several times. Dick pondered a resolution to this problem in light of budgetary restraints. He had noticed quite a few new books in his supervisor's research area, books obviously bought for personal use rather than the predetermined areas of collection development.

Dick approached his supervisor about the urgency of obtaining the new microfilm reader-printer. His supervisor said there was no money, so Dick mentioned that the books the department had been receiving did not really meet collection development standards for the area. He wondered if the supervisor knew how this happened and whether it should be reported. Dick mentioned that the estimated cost of these materials would cover the cost of replacing the old microfilm reader-printer.

Dick thus communicated his ideas for new equipment by threatening his supervisor and by appealing to the supervisor's moral and ethical standards. The use of intimidation is not an effective communication pattern, but it is sometimes used when things are not going as the low-level staff member expected.

Dick also had a wonderful idea for developing a bibliographic instruction program using a library skills workbook. He felt all freshmen students would benefit from a program concentrated on developing library skills. He and his co-workers, including his supervisor, were anxious to implement this idea for next year's freshmen class. Dick carefully documented his plan in detail and verbally highlighted it to the director. After a few weeks passed and nothing had happened, Dick mentioned his idea to a few friends in the English department, who expressed much interest. A representative from the English department then convinced the library director to implement the program. Dick thereby manipulated the situation by using external pressure to communicate his program ideas.

The lesson here for upper-level administrators is this: listen to how junior staff members communicate to you. Many junior staff members simply do not feel as if their ideas are heard. Why do they feel this way? One reason is the limited means of communicating dictated by a managing-down hierarchy. Sam E. White, John E. Dietrich, and James R. Lang indicated:

> The use of inappropriate structures, such as managing down, can lead to limited innovation capacity and low commitment or lack of staff participation in the decision-making process.[2]

Junior management can make suggestions for improvement, but an absence of reaction to ideas leads to frustration and indifference. Creativity and innovation are squelched. Junior staff members adapt to a daily routine and stop looking for ways to improve their areas. The communication pattern in a managing-down hierarchy is dehumanizing because it does not allow reaction by junior staff members; there is a strong feeling that the decision has already been made and put into place. John R. Darling and E. Dale Cluff reinforce the ideas of White, Dietrich, and Lang by indicating that junior staff members be allowed to manage up and that high-level managers be more open to ideas and willing to depart from traditional methods.[3] The influence of junior staff members on policies indicates an effective organizational structure.

The second reason that managers may not be receptive to low-level ideas is that, the more a manager lets a subordinate make decisions, the more she or he feels a loss of power or influence. Yet a junior staff member would have more respect for her or his supervisor if she or he sees that ideas are at least being considered or heard. Charles Martell stated that "more people with more power results in better productivity."[4] After all, employees would be challenged and find more meaning in their work when allowed input. Doing tasks beyond one's normal responsibilities contributes to the betterment of the organization and gives the junior member the satisfaction of having participated. Barbara Conroy and Barbara Schindler Jones find that sharing decisions, responsibilities, and work is not giving up power, but empowering others, thereby sharing power.[5] This sharing is a practical method for achieving results for the overall library program, or, to borrow a phrase, "two heads are better than one."

The third reason is that, human nature being what it is, most people are hesitant to reveal their weaknesses. Studies over the years have shown that people are often afraid to ask a reference librarian for assistance for fear of appearing ignorant. Low-level managers may suspect that high-level managers are afraid to ask junior staff members for ideas for fear of appearing uninformed regarding new technologies, new techniques, or management strategies. High-level managers often do not have time to keep up with advancement in technology and, being forced to rely on professional journals, may not have the expertise of recently graduated low-level managers. Therefore, high-level managers in the information gathering and providing industry should not ignore the experience and knowledge of low-level managers.

These three obstacles can be overcome as demonstrated by the experience of North Texas State University librarians, as cited in an article by Margaret E. Galloway. During a retreat, upper-level administrators found that junior staff members felt alienated from the decision-making process and that decisions were made without staff input. The associate director of the library suggested a project of setting up the library's budget, using three junior staff members, one clerical staff member, and the associate director. The group successfully demonstrated that they could not only handle the responsibility, but also contribute suggestions that were both creative and useful. This valuable exercise allowed many of the members to advance to higher job positions. The North Texas State University Library proved the advantages of keeping low-level management happy by using the technique of cooperative communication. In return, this library benefited from the outstanding work of its employees.[6]

The lesson is that reinforcement of their ideas and suggestions will have positive effects on the junior staff. Not all ideas will be workable, but other ideas may spring from these suggestions. Bad ideas should not be summarily dismissed, but discussed as to why they would not work. Such feedback may allow junior staff to transform the suggestion into a more feasible and workable idea. Basic communications, either via discussion or written memos, are important as a method of reinforcing the junior staff members' effectiveness within the library organization. These basic communications may include reasons why an idea would not work. For example, a suggestion may already have been unsuccessfully attempted by the organization. Taking a moment to outline why or how a particular program had been unsuccessful could benefit junior staff members who have not yet developed the "that is the way it's always been done" syndrome.

The senior staff member must be willing to take risks and be willing to learn from whomever the teacher may be. This creates a good leader model because, according to Fred M. Amram, the senior staff "must have an openness to new ideas, enjoy challenges, and must tolerate ambiguity."[7] If the low-level manager senses that a supervisor is an excellent leader model, there will be more satisfaction on the job and an increased level of performance and productivity. Energy creates more energy.

This energy can be put to good use via the principle of participative management or other management techniques that are receptive to ideas from everyone at all levels within the library organization. Using these styles of management makes work challenging and can negate problems like burnout, apathy, low morale and other attitudinal dilemmas. Mary Ann Griffin discovered that "the real difference between organizational success and failure is no doubt determined by the degree to which the library utilizes the energies and talents of its people."[8]

Supervisors should not take advantage of staff members' willingness to walk the extra mile. For example, if an employee offers to help a supervisor complete some minor tasks, the supervisor should set a limit of additional work and not continue to ask for extra help. Such action is unfair and conveys the wrong message to the remainder of the library. Nevertheless, high-level managers need to be receptive to low-level managers' ideas that may have a beneficial effect on the library organization.

References

1. Donald E. Riggs, "Leadership Is Imperative," *Technicalities* 5 (November 1985): 7–11.
2. Sam E. White, John E. Dietrich, and James R. Lang, "The Effects of Group Decision-Making Process and Problem-Situation Complexity on Implementation Attempts," *Administrative Science Quarterly* 25 (September 1980): 428–40.
3. John R. Darling and E. Dale Cluff, "Social Styles and the Art of Managing Up," *Journal of Academic Librarianship* 12 (January 1987): 350–55.
4. Charles Martell, "The Nature of Authority and Employee Participation in the Management of Academic Libraries," *College & Research Libraries* 48 (March 1987): 110–22.
5. Barbara Conroy and Barbara Schindler Jones, *Improving Communication in the Library* (Phoenix: Oryx Press, 1986), 66.
6. Margaret E. Galloway, "Introducing Junior Staff to the Administrative Process," *College & Research Libraries News* 48 (December 1987): 687–88.
7. Fred M. Amram, "Managing Innovation and Innovator," *College & Research Libraries News* 48 (November 1987): 631–32.
8. Mary Ann Griffin, "Managing Values in an Academic Library," in *Energies for Transition: Proceedings of the Fourth National Conference of the Association of College and Research Libraries*, Baltimore, Maryland, April 9–12, 1986, ed. Danuta Nitecki (Chicago: ACRL, 1986), 105–7.

3

Leadership Language: Do We Say What We Mean and Mean What We Say?

E. ANNE EDWARDS

What qualities do we look for in library leaders? Perusal of position announcements for librarians in journals or newspapers reveals advertisements for individuals with considerable library experience, professional degrees, interpersonal skills, organizational, administrative, or management skills, and the ability to communicate effectively. This last requirement is now so important that phrases such as "strong communication skills," "demonstrated ability to communicate logically, clearly, and effectively, orally and in writing," and "ability to communicate effectively essential," appear as a matter of course in library job advertisements. This insistence on communication skills reflects a genuine concern on the part of library administrators for the hiring of leaders with a commitment to communication at a time when the library world is growing and changing at such a rapid pace.

No leader works alone. Leadership entails interaction with and influence on others. Library leadership is effective if leaders work with and through the library staff, and these activities require communication. Leadership also requires constant effort on the part of the leader to ensure that the communication is clear to all involved. The communication process is a vertical, two-way system from the leaders to the staff,

19

and vice versa. Limited, poor, or one-way communication can damage the morale and effectiveness of the organization.

A facet of communication of great interest is that of language in leadership. Library leaders must communicate constantly, in different ways to different audiences. Their spoken or written communications have a variety of effects on others depending on several issues: the choice of words; the complexity of the topic; the type of audience; the use of grammar, style, and punctuation; and the moods of the communicator and the receiver. Language itself, its use and abuse by library leaders, and its effect on communication in the library setting are the subjects of this chapter.

The necessity for good communication in libraries seems, perhaps, obvious. It is stressed in consultants' reports, in annual reports, and in evaluations, yet the problem still exists. Good communication in libraries bears repeating, and evaluations of the reasons for poor communication, coupled with strategies for improvement, are still needed. The observations here address at least a part of this critical issue.

Background and Review of Literature

Work began on this topic before it was a project, due to a continuing interest in words, their meanings and derivations, and their uses in different contexts. Over the past fourteen years, examples were collected of what might be considered interesting or questionable uses of language in the profession. As the collection of examples expanded, it became clear that the topic of language, as used by library administrators, would be an important and interesting one to pursue in earnest.

Initial collection of the data was not structured and consisted of mental notes and observations. Later, written notes were taken of particularly interesting uses of language during meetings or while reading professional literature, examples of reports and memoranda to library faculty and staff were collected, and information and feedback on the topic were sought from colleagues and other members of library faculty and staff. At first it was not clear whether there would be common themes or patterns in the data, as the examples covered a multitude of issues in the use of language, but gradually themes emerged.

Manual and on-line literature searches in several indexes and abstracts—including *Library Literature*, ERIC, and LISA—on the topic of leadership language yielded very little that was pertinent. There was a wealth of information on management, administration, leadership, and supervision, as well as a vast amount of material on communication, which was, unfortunately, mostly very general in nature, saying little about language itself, and geared primarily to business, industry, and management.

Other sources of background information were found by browsing the libraries' book stacks and current periodical collections. One book, *Improving Communication in Libraries*, addressed communication of all kinds in the library setting, including a short section on language.[1] Two other titles, *Leadership on the Job* and *How We Discommunicate*, offered interesting and useful information on leadership language.[2] Many of the observations in this chapter complement the material in these last two sources.

This chapter will explore the importance of language use by library leaders and the effect of that use on the organization. Examples of specific language used by leaders will be included, as well as ideas on how library leaders might overcome some of the pitfalls of leadership language.

Need for Communication

A frequent complaint in libraries, as in other organizations, is poor communication. One department may receive information long before another, an individual may feel that he or she has been left out of the flow of information, or morale may be low in a unit where there has been verbal conflict between a supervisor and a staff member. Communication among the library staff will only be as good as the leaders who are responsible for providing and promoting that communication. Leaders must possess the skills and knowledge necessary to avoid misunderstandings, low morale, and feelings of mistrust. Their careful use of language can go far in producing a positive environment and a satisfied and productive staff.

Language can be either a bridge or a barrier. In order for it to be a bridge, there are certain skills that the library leader must master. It is not necessary for the manager to acquire a vast vocabulary, nor is it necessary to become an accomplished writer or public speaker, although these skills would not be wasted. It is easy for language usage to become a barrier, and even easier to allow it to remain so, by blaming communication problems on a particular individual and failing to investigate the reason for the breakdown.

Methods of Communication

There are numerous ways in which leaders communicate: some communications are verbal, such as oral reports, conversations, and meetings;

others are written, such as memoranda, announcements, policies and procedures, written reports, forms, and letters. The way in which language is used may vary depending on whether the communication is oral or written, and may differ also within those two methods of communication.

Oral communication frequently takes place with little formal preparation. For example, a library leader may have written notes on what he or she intends to say at a meeting, but may be caught by surprise by an impromptu question. Thus, the language that is used in reporting at a meeting may differ significantly from that used in responding to an ad hoc situation. On the other hand, there may be ample time to compose written reports or memoranda, and therefore little excuse for poor language use.

The choice of oral or written communication may depend on the type of information or on the preference of the leader or staff member. Instructions may be given in oral form, with the expectation that the receiver of those instructions will interpret and remember them correctly. When a leader perceives that a receiver consistently misunderstands an oral instruction, the tendency is for that leader to change the communication method, and issue directions in writing. This course of action may not necessarily resolve the problem. Perhaps the leader has not analyzed the situation to find that the instructions were unclear in either form.

Leaders lean toward the type of communication with which they feel most comfortable: some are content with oral interaction, with written work as a last resort; others prefer to follow up all oral communication with written memoranda or letters. There may be specific reasons for these decisions other than personal style. For example, an instruction may apply to more than one individual, and another leader should therefore be alerted. The quickest way to accomplish this communication would be through a memorandum to all parties. Documentation may also be needed for personnel reasons, or because the institution requests it in writing. Personal leadership style, however, seems to be evident in the data collected for this study. Regardless of style, it is important that the leader analyze the communication process regularly to be certain that it is effective.

The examples of language use gathered for this chapter fall into three categories: language that results in misunderstanding; language and issues of style, grammar, and punctuation; and language that requires sensitivity on the part of the leader.

Misunderstandings

Written or oral communication may result in misunderstanding for several reasons. The inclusion of library jargon or local library lingo may intimidate or confuse the receiver. A memorandum or conversation that includes a direction such as "read the shelves" or "dump the tape" could cause a new employee to panic and might result in a serious problem for the library. Situations have occurred where the receiver of the instruction "pull the cards" has followed that instruction literally, and cards have been torn out of the card catalog drawers. Library acronyms may be another source of confusion, especially for new staff. The "pc" (public catalog) may have been referred to as the "cc" (card catalog) in a previous place of employment. Careful and sensitive training of each new staff member will alleviate this problem.

Other misunderstandings due to language usage include information that appears precise but may be misinterpreted easily. The request "please pull together last year's budget figures on supplies" seems reasonable and clear on the surface, but may result in a set of figures from a different time period than the one desired. "Please pull together the figures on expenditures for supplies from October 1, 1986, to September 30, 1987," however, will almost certainly assure the delivery of correct information and will avoid the frustration, tension, and wasted time that might occur with the first example. Similar confusion may arise from the words "this week" versus "next week," or "this Friday" versus "next Friday." These terms are likely to mean different things to different people, with the result that a meeting or important deadline could be missed. Specificity in such directions will prevent many misunderstandings.

Another common pair of phrases, "as soon as possible" and "at your earliest convenience," leave both the leader and the receiver at a disadvantage. The leader may state "I need this information as soon as possible," but mean, "I need this information today," expecting the staff member to provide the information immediately, based on previous prompt response from that individual. That particular day, however, the staff member may have several other priorities, and may not realize the urgency of the request. It is clear that a potential problem such as this might be avoided if the leader gave, or the receiver requested, a precise deadline.

Style

The second area of language usage that is easily identifiable from the data is that of style, grammar, and punctuation. Library and other leaders continue to pay little attention to these issues, and in so doing, they jeopardize the communication process in their organization. Just as different leaders will have a preference for oral or written communication, they may have a preference for a particular style. Some use an informal, conversational style in most situations, changing to a more formal method of expression when external requirements come into play, such as annual, budgetary, or statistical reports. Others are more comfortable with a very formal but straightforward manner of communication, regardless of the information they are imparting. Leaders with excellent writing or oral skills reflect those skills in their communications within the library, while a few have developed a more verbose style, using longer words and complicated syntax. Of these styles, the verbose one is probably the least effective. The receiver may not be familiar with the vocabulary used by a leader with this style, and could feel threatened or insecure in working with that individual. A leader who uses vocabulary such as "herewith" for "enclosed," or "ubiquitous" for "widespread" in general library communication will probably gain the reputation of being a snob, and although some may appreciate and even emulate this style, it is more likely that staff will lose confidence in the leader's ability to communicate effectively. The leader should gear vocabulary to the audience and adapt his or her style accordingly in order to interact in a positive manner.

Jargon presents another interesting situation. It is fashionable, and sometimes more convenient, to use fad terms or constructions, such as "interface" in terms of communicating with others, or "prioritize" to mean putting things in order of importance. Although there may not be anything really wrong with using these terms, overuse should be avoided if possible. On the other hand, some phrases and words are used erroneously so often that they almost become accepted. Two examples of the most common misuse of language are the phrase "at this point in time" instead of the simple "now," and the word "irregardless" for "regardless."

We are taught never to end our sentences with prepositions, yet in oral communication it is quite common. The informal observations made during this study, however, indicated that the speakers were usually aware of the errors, and would try to correct them immediately. This behavior was evident in the majority of cases, suggesting that the speakers were aware of the rules of grammar, but could not always match the rules with the speed of the spoken word. Confusion over the use of "me" and "I" was common also, and was frequently corrected after the error was made.

Redundant phraseology in library memoranda is very common. "Very unique" is a favorite, as is "final conclusion." Although such words and phrases do not necessarily sound wrong—partly because they are used with such frequency—they are examples of poor grammatical style, and can be avoided by careful and diligent monitoring of language.

There is nothing more irritating than the receipt of a memorandum or letter with typographical errors, poor punctuation, or careless editing. An additional cost of such poor communication is that the reader may receive the content less favorably, and even look for other problems in the communication. Proofreading is time-consuming but well worth the effort; the impression is a lasting one. The advent of computers has introduced the spell-checker, an automatic program to check for spelling errors. Those responsible for communication should be sure that all written communication is checked carefully; even if a spell-checker is used, it will not identify correctly spelled words used incorrectly, such as the use of "their" for "there." Form letters prepared on computer and distributed without proofreading may contain errors resulting from information that was merged or entered incorrectly. Again, it is the library leaders who are responsible for setting an example for the rest of the organization.

Need for Sensitivity

The third problem area of leadership language that emerged from the data is that of language that requires the leaders' sensitivity. Leaders should be conscious of the morale and climate in the organization and be sensitive to the feelings of the staff. Personal names are supremely important, especially to the individuals concerned, yet how often is that importance ignored? Leaders must take the time to find out what individual staff members wish to be called and the correct spelling and pronunciation of their names. Job titles should be given the same importance. Calling a staff member by the correct name, pronouncing and spelling it correctly, and using that name in everyday conversation creates a climate of trust and improves communication. Consistently mispronouncing names or titles may indicate other problems in communication and suggest to the staff member that the leader does not consider him or her of particular importance in the organization.

Much has been made of the use of sexist or nonsexist language since the women's movement, yet the data collected revealed only one instance where the description of a library clerk included a reference to "she." Progress has been made in this area of language, and it is less of a problem now than in recent years. Nevertheless, library leaders who take positions in new geographical areas may need to listen for, and follow the established terminology for that region, regardless of the terminology with which they are familiar.

What terms should library leaders use to describe the work force in their organizations? The debate over acceptable descriptive terms for librarians and support staff continues. Librarians are called librarians, professionals, degreed librarians, faculty, information specialists, or professors. Support staff who do not hold professional degrees required by the library may be called support staff, clerks, paraprofessionals, classified staff, and even nonprofessionals or subprofessionals. Sometimes the word "staff" refers to all employees regardless of position. Use of a particular word in the wrong place can cause great unhappiness in a library, and it is extremely difficult to mend the fence once such a mistake has been made. The key to attaining high morale on the part of the staff is for library leaders to listen to the different views on this issue, and to agree on appropriate terminology that is understood by all.

The most sensitive and difficult issue in leadership language occurs in personnel evaluation. A subject that is endlessly discussed, it is one with no finite answers or directions for leaders evaluating their staff. Many evaluation systems contain imprecise or ambiguous terms that may be interpreted in completely different ways by different people. A typical system of evaluation might be a form with several questions pertaining to the individual's work performance, including quality and quantity of work, and ability to work with others and follow directions. The questions may be perfectly clear to both the leader and the staff member, but the scale on which the staff member is rated is frequently nonspecific. Generic terms such as "average," "satisfactory," "very good," or "outstanding" are commonly applied, but not always described adequately. Leaders might assist in this process by working with the rest of the staff to develop descriptive terminology or explanations of the generic terms and by insisting on clear language in such evaluations. If library leaders set an example by using specific, well-understood words and phrases in evaluations, some of the mystery and mistrust surrounding this practice might be tempered.

Language Overuse

One phrase in particular stood out from the others in the data: "As you know." Frequently used, perhaps too frequently, it may cause a negative reaction on the part of the receiver. A department head receives a memo from the director that states, "As you know, the library has decided to purchase a new microform reader. Please make sure that there is adequate space in the microforms area, as the machine will be delivered tomorrow." Imagine the reaction of the department head, who was not aware of the decision because the director had forgotten to announce it at the department heads' meeting. The innocent use of that simple phrase will certainly irritate the department head, and, if used often enough, may damage that communication line irreparably.

Receivers of information from library leaders may become annoyed by the overuse of certain phrases, such as "the library administration feels that . . . ," or "we, as a team, believe . . . ." Leaders would do well to search for new ways to express common themes, and to motivate the staff by varying the terminology for certain activities. Is it always necessary to call a committee a committee? Can we call the next committee formed a "team" or "group" or, in certain circumstances, allow the members to name themselves. In some instances leaders might find the group members would appreciate the opportunity to call themselves "The Fabulous Filers" or "The Micromasters Group." Some leaders might not feel comfortable with this unconventional approach, but trust is engendered by communicating with the staff and encouraging such independence. It is quite likely that a leader who accepts such challenges and communicates a willingness to change the established routine and vocabulary of the institution, based upon staff input, will have a supportive group of followers.

Persuasion

How do leaders encourage their staff to do their jobs? They may praise them, push them, cajole them, threaten them, or persuade them. This last method requires particular care in terms of the verbal approach chosen by the leader. For example, a staff member may be extremely busy, and yet the leader needs to have a task completed immediately. The method used to persuade this individual to change tasks may be completely different from that used with a staff member who is not as busy or is more flexible. Careful choice of words may make a significant difference, and flattery may be the best means of persuasion, as in, "I would be happy to do this myself, but your computer skills are so strong. Do you think you might be able to help me?" There may be occasions, however, when there is no time for persuasion. In these cases, the leader should make sure that the straightforward request is polite and later, upon completion of the task, that the individual is thanked for his or her assistance.

Persuasion may not always be used to request help. It may also be a tool to convince a staff member of something, or to bring that person around to thinking in the same way as the rest of a group. The language used in these situations should be planned thoughtfully since a staff member may have very strong convictions on the issue in question, and the leader will need to move slowly and gently, allowing time for the individual to express the reasons for his or her convictions and explain why they are so strong. The leader has a difficult job here, and the result may be that the persuasion will not be effective.

Falling into this category of language are expressions such as "I'd really like to see you use your expertise in this area" and "Would you consider working tonight instead of tomorrow?" Persuasion always includes an element of risk, risk that the receiver will not be persuaded and that stronger methods will be needed to convince or demand the compliance of the individual. The leader must be willing to accept that risk before embarking on persuasion. When tackling particularly difficult issues, such as persuading an entire department that they must add ten extra hours of desk hours each week with no additional personnel, the leader must make a choice between informing the group that this must be done or working with the group to explain the reasons for the change. If persuasion is likely to succeed, it should be the method of choice, since, when effectively used, it results in the receivers' acceptance of the leader's point of view and strengthens the relationship.

The examples in this chapter on language use in libraries serve to illustrate the many ways in which library leaders use language to try to communicate. The choice of a word may make the difference between acceptance and rejection of an individual by others. Consistent misuse of words will likely erode the communication process and the organization, and library leaders must be prepared to spend time on this important part of their work. Library leaders must remember that, although communication in an organization may often start in their offices, communication does not always stop at the receiver. The receiver will pass on the information through regular or informal channels. It is particularly important for leaders to communicate clearly to middle managers, who then interpret the same information to the staff. The second level of communication will be ineffective if the middle manager has not understood the information.

Planning for Good Communication

There are many techniques that are helpful in promoting good communication between leaders and their staff. The leader must plan as much as possible what he or she wishes to communicate. In doing so, the leader should consider the message that is to be conveyed, the audience, the timing, the medium through which the communication will best be delivered, and the reason for the communication. If the leader wishes to convey a message of thanks to an individual for a job well done, should it be in the form of a letter, a pat on the back while strolling through the library, or a note in the library newsletter? Once the medium has been selected, the style and vocabulary should fall into place. This type of planning may seem cumbersome and time consuming initially, but with practice and time it will become natural. Planning is the mark of an effective leader and a good communicator.

Good communication on the part of a leader also means low ego involvement. A strong but sensitive leader will not only talk to and inform the staff, but will also listen to the upward communication and ask for feedback on the communication process. This may be difficult for a strong leader, especially when the topic of conversation is one where there is disagreement between the leader and the staff. Library leaders are often at a disadvantage because of the general feeling of mistrust of administrators; anything leaders can do to dispel that feeling will enhance the prospects of improving communication, and the use of language is one of the most important skills in a library leader.

Leaders will be known as good communicators if they avoid language that may be easily misunderstood, use good grammar and clear style, and are sensitive to the feelings of their staff in their communications.

How often we hear the words, "that's not quite what I meant." We need to work harder to avoid misunderstandings. There are no easy ways to overcome our deficiencies in communication. We must practice and be constantly aware of the effect we have on others through our language and thus the expression of our meaning.

Conclusion

These observations on the use of leadership language serve to illustrate a few ways in which library leaders communicate or fail to communicate with their staff and colleagues. Library leaders need to be aware of the power of language and the ways in which it influences others, both positively and negatively. Although there has been much written on communication in general, there is still little research on the specific language use, and few, if any, studies on the short- and long-range effect of leadership language on the receiver. Strong leadership is essential in the library field, and yet, curiously, there is a gap in our knowledge and research on language use that needs to be filled. Perhaps these observations will at least encourage library leaders to listen to themselves and to successful leaders in order to improve. Finally, library and other leaders might wish to follow the suggestion of Joseph Pulitzer, who stated, "Put it before them briefly so they will read it, clearly so they will understand it, picturesquely so they will remember it, and, above all, accurately so they will be guided by its light."

References

1. Barbara Conroy and Barbara Schindler Jones, *Improving Communication in the Library* (Phoenix: Oryx Press, 1986).
2. William K. Fallon, ed., *Leadership on the Job: Guides to Good Supervision*, 3d ed. (New York: AMACOM, 1981); Philip Lesly, *How We Discommunicate* (New York: AMACOM, 1979).

4

The Landscape of Leadership

BARBARA B. FISCHLER

If one is to lead, one must lead through something to something else. Any discussion of leadership cannot ignore these two realities. Most of us are fairly certain about our goals; we are probably much less certain about the "through," or the landscape through which we travel as we attempt to lead. I shall offer a description of the landscape as I perceive it—a description offered as the beginning of an inquiry. Most certainly it is not the complete answer.

As professionals, and as scholars, we talk about our collegiality and our "peerness." Most of us work in institutions that are predominantly democratic, in a society that is a democracy. We attempt to live by a code that stresses equality; yet we seek leaders who can emerge, excel, serve as models, and motivate others. We face a dilemma Alexis de Tocqueville described when he looked at the America of the 1830s and saw much the same landscape we work in today.

> When the conditions of men are almost equal, they do not easily allow themselves to be persuaded by one another. As they all live in close inter-course, as they have learned the same things together, and as they lead the same life, they are not naturally disposed to take one of themselves

for a guide and to follow him implicitly. Men seldom take the opinion of their equal or of a man like themselves upon trust.[1]

If we go to the literature of management for models that will help us lead people, there are three commonly known descriptive models available: organizational, industrial engineering, and behavioral science. They are summarized and critiqued by Frederick Herzberg in his article "One More Time: How Do You Motivate Employees?"[2] The "eternal triangle" of personnel management models that Herzberg discusses are tools with which we try to lead our professionals, clerical staff, and volunteers. He distinguishes between two key terms: "motivation" and "movement." Careless use of the eternal triangle can lead to a great deal of movement but little true motivation. Herzberg maintains that "motivation encompasses passion; movement is sterile."[3] He shows how each of these personnel theories has succeeded and failed and discusses some of the successes of job enrichment and how to accomplish these through motivating when feelings are not excluded.

If motivation means generating enthusiasm, how does one best do that? How does one focus feeling and attention on a goal? Another answer comes to us from the nineteenth century: Ralph Waldo Emerson, discussing the power of art, said that the power of the orator, artist, and leader depends on the depth of the artist's insight of that object he contemplates. Emerson further stated:

> It is the habit of certain minds to give an all-excluding fullness to the object, the thought, the word they alight upon, and to make that for the time the deputy of the world. These are the artists, the orators, the leaders of society. The power to detach and to magnify by detaching is the essence of rhetoric in the hands of the orator and the poet.[4]

Our object of contemplation is human behavior in the workplace. Taking a cue from Erving Goffman, I shall investigate the people in our landscape as they communicate in two ways: expressions given and expressions given off. According to Goffman the "nonverbal, presumably unintentional kind" of expression is a "more theatrical and contextual kind" of communication that can help us understand those whom we would lead.[5]

One of the most important elements of leadership is communication. Most individuals accept communication as basic and simple, an activity in which we are all engaged throughout our lives. However, communication is probably one of the most difficult, misused, and misunderstood activities in which we engage. Differences in personality types and experiences create barriers that interfere with the messages that pass from the sender to the receiver.

The invention of the Myers-Briggs Type Indicator made it possible for us to learn about various temperament styles of individuals with whom we are interacting. It was found that there are sixteen basic types and thirty-two mixed types of personalities. The four pairs that make up these types are:

E (extraversion)	*I* (introversion)
S (sensing)	*N* (intuitive)
T (thinking)	*F* (feeling)
P (perceiving)	*J* (judging)

Each one of these type preferences will have a basic attitude or behavior pattern and tends frequently to use words or phrases indicative of this type of preference.

Let us examine briefly each of the types and the vocabulary one expects this type of individual to use:

E: Extravert. This type of person has considerable energy, is social, and is frequently engaged in lively conversation. Typical words used include: *extensive, very, much, interaction, multiple, action.*

I: Introvert. This type of person is more territorial, private, and meditative, and less energetic. Typical words used include: *concentration, limited, internal, intense, conservative.*

S: Sensing. This type of person is the practical individual. Typical words used include: *sensible, actual, realistic, facts.*

N: Intuitive. This type of person is usually an innovator. Typical words used include: *inspiration, imagination, possible, fascinating.*

T: Thinking. This type of person appears to be objective and impersonal. Typical words used include: *analysis, firm, policy, standards.*

F: Feeling. This type of person is emotional and sensitive. Typical words used include: *humane, sympathy, soft.*

P: Perceiving. This type of person is considered to be flexible. Typical words used include: *adaptable, tentative, wait, open.*

J: Judging. This type of individual is decisive. Typical words used include: *settled, planned, urgent, decided.*[6]

There are words that project feelings that both the sender and the receiver should notice that help to identify the true message. These words express feelings such as anger, fear, inadequacy, love, happiness, caring, and adequacy (annoyed, embarrassed, powerless, amiable, pleased, kind, secure).[7]

Communication styles of individuals center around four types of indicators: *SP, SJ, NT,* and *NF.* Communication characteristics of these temperaments are:

SP—ease in verbalizing; commendation
SJ—theme of caution; thoroughness
NT—assumption of understanding; technical and terse
NF—caring and optimistic; enthusiasm[8]

A leader may come from any of the temperament styles. What is mandatory is for the leader to know himself or herself and to be able to recognize the type of individual with whom he or she is interacting. The primary job of the leader then becomes understanding and appreciating the style of the individual and communicating both verbally and nonverbally in a manner that will achieve the results he or she wishes to obtain.

How does a leader employ the information about types to achieve this optimal communication? How does one articulate visions and values as well as facts in order to influence, to motivate, to exercise power, to engage in controversy, and to reach both the individual as well as a heterogenous constituency?

To accomplish leadership there are still two important elements of this landscape that must be employed: listening and the proper use of the nonverbal climate.

Listening is an art frequently neglected and sometimes confused with hearing. The components of effective listening are

1. a true intention to listen,
2. concentration on the sender's message,
3. control of your emotions, and
4. checking for understanding only when invited to do so and in a constructive manner.

One can listen in each of the styles (*S, N, T, F*) employing the best traits of each. Flavil R. Yeakley, Jr., summarizing his research in psychological-type communication, succinctly describes the ways as follows:

> The sensing style means interpreting at a very practical level and asking such questions as:
>> What is the speaker saying?
>> How should the words be decoded?
>> How should the message be perceived?
> The intuitive style means understanding at a much deeper level and asking such questions as:
>> What does the speaker really mean?
>> What are the assumptions underlying the message?

What are the implications of the message?
What are the possibilities suggested by the message?
The thinking style means analyzing and organizing while asking such questions as:
What is the structure of the message?
What is the central idea?
What are the main points?
What are the subpoints?
How are the various points related?
Is there adequate evidence to justify each claim?
Is the reasoning logical?
Are the claims true or false?
The feeling style means evaluating and appreciating while asking such questions as:
What values are suggested by the message?
Should these values be accepted or rejected?
How do I feel about the message?
How do I feel about the speaker?[9]

In summary, it becomes obvious that each personality type has its own language and listening style. Mismatches result in impaired communication. To be understood well on a one-to-one basis, both the sender and the receiver must be using the same communication style.

Try testing yourself. Tape record a presentation for a particular personality type and ask a person of that type to summarize what you have said. What is the result? Did you make your message clear for that person?

The last element of the landscape is the nonverbal climate, better known in the literature today as "body language." To communicate effectively, you must pay attention to the cues and signals given off by gestures and body positioning—both yours and the receiver's.

To present a positive, friendly, and supportive climate, use these techniques:

Body
Establish a comfortable distance
Be relaxed
Lean forward
Copy the receiver's body movements
Keep your posture as open as possible

Head
Tilt your head forward or to the side
Turn your face toward the receiver
Make eye contact, but do not stare longer than a few seconds

Nod your head vertically (if appropriate as affirmation for the receiver)

Use facial expressions that indicate involvement and responsiveness

Arms
Hold your palms up
Keep your arms loose at your side
Keep your fingers still
Touch the receiver if appropriate

Legs
If you cross your legs, cross toward receiver
Use gestures natural for you

Feet
If standing, place your feet as parallel as possible (inward indicates subordination)
Stand relatively still

Voice
Make your vocal tone and speed of delivery as soft, low-pitched, and slow as is comfortable

The opposites of these techniques will tend to create a defensive climate, one that suggests that you are not listening with acceptance and empathy, or that you are not listening at all. Deliberate use of negative techniques sends the receiver an "I can't be bothered with you" message.

No leader is perfect and no leader will be successful in sending or receiving the correct message every time. What is vital is to be able to recognize the failures and to adjust the situation as quickly and adroitly as possible.[10]

Few leaders reach historical stature. There are many fine leaders on a less-famous scale whom each of us has known or will know. Many of these individuals have a "code" through which they lead. I have had the pleasure of working for an administrator whose leadership on the local scale is superb and who has such a "code"—Howard G. Schaller, our executive dean and the director of our Center on Philanthropy. He is a person who uses all of the communication skills to near perfection while living and administrating by and through three points:

There is never a crisis.
Be your own scorekeeper.
Never tire of doing good.

Mastery of the three components of the leadership landscape takes work. You arrive at this by

1. learning to know yourself and your "type";
2. learning to know those with whom you interact;
3. developing excellent listening skills;
4. making use of the appropriate nonverbal climate;
5. making a conscious effort to adapt yourself to reach the receiver;
6. using all of this knowledge with *honesty* to establish *trust*.

References

1. Alexis de Tocqueville, *Democracy in America*, vol. 2 (New York: Alfred A. Knopf, 1966), 354–55.
2. Frederick Herzberg, "One More Time: How Do You Motivate Employees?" *Harvard Business Review* 65 (September–October 1987): 109–20.
3. Ibid., 120.
4. Ralph Waldo Emerson, "Essays: First Series," *The Complete Works of Ralph Waldo Emerson*, vol. 2 (New York: AMS Press, 1968), 354–55.
5. Erving Goffman, *The Presentation of Self in Everyday Life* (Woodstock, N. Y.: Overlook Press, 1973), 4.
6. David Keirsey and Marilyn Bates, *Please Understand Me: An Essay on Temperament Styles* (Del Mar, Calif.: Prometheus Nemesis Books, 1978), 13.
7. Andrew D. Wolvin and Carolyn Gwynn Coakley, *Listening*, 2d ed. (Dubuque: William C. Brown, 1985), 217–19.
8. Keirsey and Bates, *Please Understand Me*, 131–53.
9. Flavil R. Yeakley, Jr., "Implications of Communication Style Research for Psychological Type Theory," *Research in Psychological Type* 6 (1983): 22–23.
10. For an excellent summary of the elements of leadership and for thought-provoking background reading, see John W. Gardner's *Leadership Papers*, numbers 1–8 (Washington, D.C.: Independent Sector, 1986–87). The National Institute of Business Management's *Personal Report for the Executive* is a semimonthly publication that offers continuing, helpful reminders about interpreting behavioral clues and listening well. The Gardner papers and the *Personal Report* were helpful to me in this project and continue to help in my work as an administrator.

5

The Language of Library Leadership: Effective Communication

Charles D. Hanson

"I don't know what you mean by *your* way," said the Queen, "all the ways about here belong to me . . . ."

Lewis Carroll

The Concept of Leadership Communication

Perhaps no area of library leadership receives so much criticism as the area of communication. Demands for better communication among and within library departments, for more openness between personnel and the director, and for greater input into the dynamics of the library organization occur frequently in libraries. Quite often the feeling is that library leaders speak like the Queen of Hearts, communicating from the top down. How can we provide for better library communication without a loss of privacy, the creation of a paper-cluttered world, or a world of endless chatter? How, too, can we prevent the abuse of communication, which could turn it to bad ends? As one of Shakespeare's characters states, "The abuse of greatness is when it disjoins/remorse from power." Certainly improved communication must be a goal of every effective library leader. Many of us remember the words spoken by the prison warden in the movie *Cool Hand Luke*: "What we have here is a failure to communicate." This failure to communicate is reflected in the business world where the estimates for the costs of ineffective communication range as high as one hundred billion dollars a year.[1]

Library communication is essentially no different from other types of business communication. It is a *human* act involving a sender (speaker) and receiver (listener). It is a dynamic act, interactive, and, when most effective, based on dialogue which in turn creates a proper action. It is a given that communication does not exist in a vacuum but is part of a social matrix. A library is a human communications network, with library personnel who have different habits, needs, attitudes, and abilities. As the pressures of technology, funding, networking, and staff evaluation become more extreme, the necessity for effective communication in libraries becomes more pronounced. Communication is a forum for the articulation of concepts, one that permits, in the words of the poet Gerard Manley Hopkins, the articulation of "all things counter, original, spare . . . ." Its importance cannot be emphasized enough, for as Herbert S. White has pointed out, "Communication shortcomings lie at the root of the great majority of management problems."[2]

Multidimensional Approaches to Effective Leadership Communication

Librarians are not the only professional group these days talking about leadership and communication, though it is commonly accepted that every library job description emphasizes communication as a job requirement. For example, a recent study of school principals noted that 60 to 70 percent of a principal's daily activities "fell under the heading of communicating . . . and that these interactions were informal, brief, and fragmented . . . few exchanges were longer than ten minutes."[3] Within a library leader's day, frequent interruptions seem to be the fare of every sender. As a result of these interruptions, communication exchanges may become muddled. The receiver frequently takes away mixed messages.

Consultant Kenneth H. Blanchard maintains that if the sender wishes to influence in an effective way, that person must concentrate on the behavior of the receiver. He points out that there are two types of behavior. *Directive behavior* is a one-way communication in which the leader tells the followers "what to do, where to do it, when to do it, and how to do it. The three operative words for directive behavior are *structure, control,* and *supervise.*" *Supportive behavior* permits the leader to engage in two-way communication, which "provides support and encouragement; facilitates interaction; and involves the followers in decision making. The three operative words for supportive behavior are *praise, listen,* and *facilitate.*"[4]

Leaders with effective communication skills have long known that it is important to vary the communication style to the situation. An administrator presenting a proposal for a new computer system to a board of trustees utilizes a different approach than the library administrator who is counseling a staff member. A library director explaining a library policy to a disgruntled patron speaks with a style different from that used in speaking with a maintenance person about the procedure of setting up the meeting room.

The leadership style of communication may vary between the two approaches, directive or supportive, resulting in the message that is most effective for that situation; at its most basic, "different strokes for different folks," according to a leader's modus operandi. Management consultant Clayton Sherman cautions, however, that "some people literally do not understand what it is you're saying. You can tell them there's a problem—and internally they are not going along, even though they might be nodding their heads."[5] He notes that standards of performance must be communicated. Likewise, "selling the library program" remains one of the tests of the efficacy of a library leader's communication skills.

Therefore, it is essential that the denotative and connotative value of the words chosen when relaying a message be clear and precise. The sender's obligation is to make the message understandable! It is never the receiver's responsibility to interpret the message. For example, I once had a difficult time getting my message across to a staff secretary who insisted on placing her office chair and desk in a position with her back toward anyone who came into the office. Only after I had explained the consequences of her furniture arrangement—that the person entering the room felt ignored, that there was not a friendly recognition of service—did she modify her pattern and move her desk to face the public.

Less Is More When Communicating Leadership Ideas

Improved communication should be a stated goal of library leaders. Some leaders interpret this to mean more is better: more meetings, more memos ("more M&M's" as one of my staff calls them). More meetings and memos, however, are often not effective communications. The library leader who rules by memos, who continues to drone on at staff meetings—the constant verbalizer—is less effective than the leader who is succinct. Overemphasis on structure and "the last word" can make policies and procedures nothing more than cumbersome documentation rather than staff-generated input and ownership. There is also the danger of getting too caught up in verbalizing, leaving little time left to actually *do* anything.

Effective communication, like management, may lie in the process of gaining control by giving up control, a Zen-like concept. This presupposes, however, a level of sophistication on the part of the communication leader. Most library leaders simply "give up" or "give in" to pressure. When the stakes are high, when demands must be met, and when deadlines are imminent, direct communication becomes even more important in one's routines. Yet nothing is as simple as it seems, most notably a command of effective communication skills. As the English poet Robert Graves stated, " A cool web of language winds us in."

Streamlining Library Communication for Empowerment

How is communication to be streamlined? How do we simplify structure and eliminate bureaucratic rules? Communication, when initiated at the top, allows for responsibility for the action of that communication at the grass roots level, where true empowerment occurs. This action is reflected in site-based budgeting, for example, where each library department is given responsibility for making decisions about budget as close to the environment in which it occurs as possible. Some communication experts maintain that "the manager's job is to establish the boundaries around a fairly broad space. The individual's responsibility is to find the best way of doing things within that space."[6] Hence the productivity and service of a reference department are tied to the empowered individuals working within that department who assume ownership for the outcome of the work.

It probably does little good, however, for library leaders to express their belief in *empowerment* when the accompanying resources are not provided. The technical services department needs a budget that will permit them to carry out their functions; the reference department must have a top-notch reference collection in order to provide excellent service.

Language, too, should be streamlined and precise. Clear, precise speech discourages flip-flopping on an issue and encourages the use of language to bring the truth to light. Streamlined communication can be compared to a haiku poem, whose beauty and meaning lie in its compressed form; more words would lessen its meaning and impact. A control of diction is a search for the right word with the exact meaning, of not putting words between the truth and ourselves. Far too often, those who have nothing of substance to communicate practice the art of rhetoric. Library leaders know that they are responsible for promoting the library as an information-rich resource. The statement has been made that our society is information-rich but knowledge-poor (one of the premises of Theodore Roszak's book *The Cult of Information*). When it comes to clear, potent communication skills, the volume of words has little to do with the motivation toward action described by the message. If library leaders can communicate quickly as well as clearly, the action will occur in a more timely manner and will lead to streamlined performance. It does not mean that communication will necessarily occur even with the right information. What do we want? "Just the facts, ma'am, just the facts," without any negative connotations.

Leadership Communication: A Vision of Delight

Clarity of words and communication of vision are inseparable. Every library leader communicates a sense of purpose and direction—either verbally or nonverbally. One business leader asserts that "sharing of vision is the highest principle of management. That is leadership."[7] But good leadership involves delivering a message in a timely manner, with the end result being a call for action ending in results. Should the leader overstate the message, the vision of the message may be lost. What is the *vision* being communicated? The secret to effective communication, as in good salesmanship, is to get the message across with no negativity involved. What type of message must library leaders deliver in order to motivate library staff toward excellence of service and product?

Library leaders sell the vision of effective, productive library systems almost exclusively through communication. In a sense, all communication is "in process," for it means constant rethinking and reevaluating. This communication brings vision into focus. Great leaders communicate a vision: the American Library Association president communicates the direction of ALA; leadership forums present opinions on what candidates for office wish to offer the membership (including ALA presidential candidates offering their vision of ALA's future).

Linked indelibly with vision is a sense of perspective. Perspective is a capability that comes with experience but is a necessary, expected quality of library leadership. There is a basic energy born out of the creative power of perspective—that of ideas, of trust, and of integrity. However, many leaders do not lead; they simply follow staff or public opinion. Effective leaders are "not necessarily popular; they want to take us somewhere, and some of us don't necessarily want to go there."[8] The race is not necessarily to the swift, but to the sensible. Lewis Carroll wrote in *Alice's Adventures in Wonderland,* "take care of the sense and the sounds will take care of themselves."

Library personnel not only want a vision, but want a vision they can respect. For too long the vision that library personnel have had of library leaders has been tarnished by those leaders' inability to give clearly directed instructions, to convey information precisely, to make requests that result in timely action or, in some cases, to communicate library needs to the outside world. It would certainly appear that a darkening of the vision was brought home in 1984 when the U. S. Department of Education issued *A Nation at Risk* without any mention of the library's role in national education. True, library leaders quickly responded with *Alliance for Excellence,*[9] but it seemed to have arrived too late to bolster some of our confidence in both library leadership and effective communication skills.

Fortunately, some library leaders have recovered from that sin of omission. For example, Marilyn L. Miller presented her powerful statement on the importance of school library media centers to a senate subcommittee.[10] Library leaders now participate in the annual Library Legislative Day in Washington, D.C. More are unafraid to speak of library ideals and readers' rights—witness Judith Krug of the ALA Intellectual Freedom Office—rather than give in to the censor, to fail to uphold free access to libraries, or to base decisions on whimsy or fashion.

There is always a danger, in spite of the Library of Congress's massive presence in Washington, D.C., that our national library vision will not be communicated. James Madison once wrote

> a popular government without popular information, or the means of acquiring it, is but a prologue to a Farce or a Tragedy; or, perhaps both. Knowledge will forever govern ignorance, and a people who mean to be their own governors must arm themselves with the power which knowledge gives.

Effectively controlled, positively reinforced communication is that power.

Effective Leadership Communication: Simplified or Simplistic?

If there is one basic precept about effective library communication, it is that the message must be simplified, not simplistic. We in libraryland still go around speaking a type of Orwellian Newspeak. We speak of retrospective conversion (as though it were a new religion), of COM catalogs, of CD-ROM and other technology and assume that we are communicating. To a large extent we are—with ourselves. For a time, some library staff saw the designation MARC and asked, "MARC who?" Certainly no profession is without its list of buzzwords. Techies speaking computerese ("Now try a cold boot") are often viewed as the leaders in their profession, and perhaps these are the people who indeed guide our destinies. But there is a need for enhanced communication that is effectively intelligible. K.I.S.S., the acronym for "*keep it simple, stupid*," is a helpful, if at times humbling, reminder.

The use of jargon and the growing reliance on computers have created a communication block. The use of technological words or jargon impedes the flow of effective messages; it adds nothing to the information being shared and may indeed prevent any decisive action being taken by the receiver. The computer distances us from the source. Leaders may treat staff members in the same way that they treat the cold mechanics of technology, taking little note of personal feelings or conditions. Worse, relying on technological language may foster a solution that is at once too simplistic and totally at odds with an understanding of the humanistic services and the human complexities so necessary for effective library communication.

Communication by Listening

Yet the goal of speaking the truth, which is the purpose of all libraries, should not be forgotten. Up to this point we have been speaking of the leader as a good sender of messages. Being a good listener is the other essential part of communication and should not be forgotten. Thomas Jefferson was fond of saying, "Here [at the University of Virginia] we are not afraid to follow truth wherever it may lead, nor to tolerate any error so long as reason is left free to combat it." The library leader is a truth seeker, and a listener, someone who delays responses until the facts are clearly understood. In a survey conducted by Padgett-Thompson in 1985, one thousand respondents were asked to name the three qualities of a good boss that enhanced on-the-job satisfaction. The results demonstrated that 27 percent wanted a boss who provided freedom for independent action (the sense of empowerment mentioned earlier), while 23 percent noted that an ideal boss "listens to staff, is accessible, has open-door policy."[11]

The key to powerful communication lies in listening. Or, as one library director remarked, "I communicate by listening." It takes, however, a sense of security to communicate by listening. Moreover, it takes a sense of self and knowledge of what good leadership is all about. John Heider points out that "enlightened leadership is service, not selfishness. The leader grows more and lasts longer by placing the well-being of all above the well-being of self alone. Paradox: by being selfless, the leader enhances self." [12] One need only read the program offerings for conferences to see that "How to Deal with a Problem Boss" is a popular subject because many library leaders do not have the communication skills to listen effectively. A good listener is one who not only hears what is being said but also understands what is being stated, both verbally and nonverbally, a process known as metacommunications.

Communicating the Leadership Message: I Am Able

In order for communication to be effective it must be the following:

Understandable: The intent of the speaker must be easily understood, with no buzzwords, jargon, or unclear messages.

Believable: The communication must be acceptable to the personal value system (credibility) of the speaker and of the listener. There must be no sense of power seeking; only the message is the medium.

Achievable: Communication should encourage creativity and discourage negativity. It should be positive in its intent and action; success-oriented. Many library workers fall back on worn phrases ("We've tried that before"; "it won't work here") when a goal seems unobtainable.

Desirable: Does this fit with the concept of library service? Will it be worth doing? Does it promote a sense of self-worth in the process?

Controllable: Communication is *directed* speech. It is not random, sporadic, or nonsensical. It should have impact and power; it would be timely and not wasteful of energy. It must use established channels of communication. It should encourage participation and feedback and discourage responses such as, "I was caught off guard," or, "I was blindsided." It should not have a revenge motive.

All these terms convey a sense of *able*; that is, I can do (it).

Everyone wants to communicate effectively, but often we are too busy or too distracted to achieve that desired end. Peter Drucker has noted that "if there is any one 'secret' of effectiveness, it is concentration. Effective executives do first things first and they do one thing at a time."[13] So too with communication. Effective communication skills require a logical progression of thought. The receiver of the message must feel that acting on the message will create a sense of pride, and self-esteem and will avoid conflict. The receiver must believe that by proceeding expeditiously it is self-actualizing (to use Abraham Maslow's theory of human motivation) to perform the stated request.

Communicating Leadership Expectations: What Did You Say—What Did You Mean?

Communication that is misdirected or misunderstood can be problematic. Note, for example, this invitation to a fine arts program: "You may pick the tickets up either the day of the event or the day prior, whichever comes first."[14] Would we be surprised to "hear ourselves as others hear us?"

Of course the use of obtuse language is also a barrier. Most things printed by the U.S. government are impossible to understand. "A Bureaucrat's Guide to Chocolate Chip Cookies," which asks the baker to "associate key chocolate and nut subsystems and execute stirring operations," is an excellent example of obfuscation.[15] Then there is the Iowa farmer who wrote the county commissioner to find out if a paint he was going to use was safe. The commissioner provided a series of obscure, jargon-filled responses; e.g., "Temporal necessities predicate that application be neutralized negatively." After lengthy correspondence because of the farmer's inability to understand the message, the correspondence culminated in a final, precise message from the commissioner: "Don't use it. It eats the hell out of your pipes."[16]

Too often the communication in libraries comes in after the fact, when a staff member must be reprimanded for not achieving a desired result. Staff members not only need to be spoken to and listened to, but they expect clear direction and guidance when performing tasks. No wonder so many say, "I didn't know that is what you wanted; tell me what you want." As Herbert S. White points out, "It is not usually their actions or decisions that get managers into difficulty with staff members . . . it is a failure to explain, a failure to specify intent and a failure to convince others that decisions have been carefully thought out."[17] No library leader should settle for less than top-notch performance, but no leader should expect that performance without precise communications.

Consultant Robert Half believes that it is important to "spell out assignments" and "publicize company goals."[18] Library leaders, busy with day-to-day demands, often forget that the unproductive work may be unproductive because the job responsibilities are not clear. If tardiness on the job is a problem, the simple solution may be to say, "Be on time!" but the effective communication is far more involved than that brief directive. Communication must make the corrective behavior a desired action through positive reinforcement, not fear of punishment or reward. Any library leader knows that the most important person in the organization is the happy, satisfied, productive employee. One of the signals of an unproductive environment, Half notes, is "any sudden and substantial rise—or decline—in the amount of communication between employees and management."[19]

Communication on Both Sides of the Brain: Humor and Participatory Management

Frequently, scant attention is paid to both the reasoning (cognitive) and the emotional (affective) content of communication. When library leaders are convinced of the importance of their "mission"—providing and promoting library services to everyone—the resulting communication is directed to the cognitive side of the brain. The result is often rigid, narrowly focused, serious, and dull. Instead of appealing to curiosity, openness, experimentation, and innovation, the appeal is often stoic, self-contained, and tough.

Norman D. Stevens, an academic library director, places great value on humor and creativity. "The careful and appropriate use of humor can . . . go a long way towards creating a climate in which creative and innovative ideas have a better chance of being put forward and given serious consideration."[20] Effectively controlled levity can ease tension and provide a release value for any strained communication. This technique encourages staff to understand the message in a positive atmosphere.

In addition, more attention is being paid to the role of participatory management, which provides communication channels for staff involvement in decision making. Libraries are now involving all levels of staff, in the form of advisory committees, to promote better communications, both intragroup and interdepartmental. One of these examples occurred at North Texas State University, where junior staff members were introduced to the administrative process;[21] another took place at Tulsa Public Library, where staff were asked to share in the budgeting process.[22]

This involvement through participatory management provides a heightened sense of responsibility for completion of tasks (empowerment) and for the fulfillment of a staff member's set of values and beliefs. It allows communication to occur at many levels, avoiding "the rules for stifling innovation,"[23] which are described in Rosabeth Moss Kanter's book *The Change Masters*. Good communication must appeal to both sides of the brain. There must be opportunity for risk taking, creativity, and innovation.

Library Team Building through Communication: Leading by Example

Effective communication must be based on trust and the establishment of trust so that responsibilities can be delegated and the development of the library's most valuable resource—its staff—can occur. The leader must be capable of conveying clarity and vision so that the overall mission and goals of the organization are articulated in a way that everyone on the library team understands. That trust is conveyed by delegation and empowerment. More often, *how* a person is told is as important as *what* the person is told. The one word summing up communication delivery is *attitude*. Clement Stone stated that "there is little difference in people, but that little difference makes a big difference. The little difference is attitude, and the big difference is whether it is positive or negative." Herbert S. White confirms that attitude is important: "Intragroup communication is subject to a number of factors, including jealousies and rivalries, conflicts over authority, and the fear that good ideas are stolen if freely divulged."[24]

With massive changes occurring within libraries, technological automation being the major one, it is understandable why staff may oppose change. Jay E. Daily has studied many of the conflicts that evolve in the area of library automation. He notes that "the major difficulty of any kind of administration is summed up in the word *communication*."[25] In short, an effective leader must be able to get everyone working together, rather than at cross-purposes.

How do leaders take risks? Better yet, how do leaders communicate to others that it is important to take risks? Quite often library leaders are not willing to be controversial. Many want to rest secure in a point of view that cannot be disputed, attacked, or controverted. Many fall for easy compromise or, worse yet, expediency, to achieve the end product. Many wait for consensus, rather than being a molder of consensus. Or some wait until all action is "killed in a committee." A few may not even profit from the self-knowledge gained by experimentation and thus rob themselves of the opportunity to know themselves and other library staff members through discourse and dialogue. Perhaps many are not astute problem solvers or good listeners because of distractions with anticipated future problems or cares. As the poet William Wordsworth wrote, "The world is too much with us, late and soon, / getting and spending, we lay waste our powers." A great leader need not feel that power has laid waste when that power is perceived as effective by the staff who must carry out that action.

In the September 1987 issue of *College & Research Libraries*, a number of articles addressed the issue of "What Professional Librarians Expect from Administrators." One librarian provided a list of thirteen qualities (stability, leadership, and others), remarking that "in the course of providing leadership, an administrator should not penalize a librarian who may disagree with him or her" because "fear is the worse element that can be unleashed in an organization."[26] Another librarian noted that "the ideal leader is above all a model."[27] Finally, a library administrator notes that "getting librarians and administrators to view their respective roles realistically and work together constructively in a collegial, congenial, trusting partnership would seem to be the top priority."[28] This blending of qualities in the ideal library leader hedges on one very important quality: the ability to communicate effectively. These qualities prevent communication by crisis, i.e., "If there is a crisis, we communicate." Crisis management leads to reactionary and divisive factions, distrust and fear, and misunderstandings.

Leadership Communication Skills: Motivation, Values, and Time

Library leadership must provide the working environment and communication channels that provide for good motivation. Leaders can communicate motivation through money, promotion, prestige, recognition, or praise. Yet according to a recent survey by Wyatt Company Consultants, fewer than 50 percent of American workers think their bosses properly motivate them, provide regular feedback, or solve "people problems."[29] Pushing and pulling library staff does not work; an open, receptive atmosphere where the library worker experiences self-worth does work.

Stuart M. Schmidt and David Kipnis identify four types of communicators: *shotguns* (those who "refuse to take no for an answer"); *tacticians* (those who actively try to influence others, relying on reason and logic); *ingratiators* (active persuaders, relying on flattery); and *bystanders* (those who seldom influence, but stand by watching the action).[30] Schmidt and Kipnis assert that there are different combinations of communication methods, not just being "overly assertive as the best tactic." Reason, friendliness, coalition, higher authority, and bargaining also work. They conclude, for example, that the shotgun method "has its long-range costs, including less favorable evaluation, lower salaries, more job tension and greater personal stress." Another article maintains that the twenty-first-century executive will need "a double dollop of moxie and charisma . . . must be less a commander than a coach who 'converts people and persuades them to share values.' "[31] Library leaders must make those values clear and *shared*.

Effective communication leaders must know the importance of time. Peter Drucker points out that leaders "do not start with tasks. They start with their time."[32] He encourages leaders to know personal limits. Just how much time is there to communicate? Demands on time can lead to exhaustion and fatigue, which in turn impede communication skills, sometimes diluting the message, or creating a sense of futility. It can lead to abrupt messages, like the characters speaking in Samuel Beckett's *Waiting for Godot*: Estragon: I can't go on like this. / Vladimir: That's what you think.

Library Communication: Evaluating Performance

No area of library leadership is as troublesome as staff evaluation and the evaluation of job performance. Yet staff evaluations involve communication, often the one opportunity to provide the criticism and praise that can result in better job performance. Jonathan A. Lindsey has written that "performance evaluation generates more anxiety in an organization than any other single event during the year."[33] Most library leaders seem torn about giving the right combination of praise and criticism. Consultant Kenneth Blanchard points out that "giving an equal amount of praise and criticism may not be enough to save you from being thought of as a bad boss. In most groups, there's a need for four times as many positive interactions—that is, praisings—as negative interactions."[34]

Sheila D. Creth, in *Effective On-the-Job Training: Developing Library Human Resources*, has developed an extensive review of library training, pointing out the need for a communication model that avoids sending conflicting messages, one that recognizes that "non-verbal behavior always carries the most powerful message between people."[35] Praise and success are effective communication motivators in libraries as well as in business. There was a time when MBO (Management By Objectives) was accepted as the one operative standard for determining staff evaluations as well as library operations, but this method may have its communication pitfalls because of its rigidity and therefore may not always lead to success.[36] The effective leader provides an opportunity for staff success (better evaluations) by communicating positive reinforcement to create the desired behavior.

A Library Communication Model:
Learning through Awareness

G. K. Chesterton wrote, "It isn't that they can't see the solution. It is that they can't see the problem." Does this sound familiar in most libraries? Much can be learned about communication models by looking at teaching models. For example, the teaching research of Madeline Hunter, a foremost expert on teacher-learner behavior, offers a teaching model:[37]

1. The objective: Is the message to be conveyed to the receiver clear? Hunter notes that it is inexcusable to arrive at a staff meeting asking, "What are we going to talk about today?"
2. Input: What information is needed by the receiver (listener) in order to achieve the objective? Is special training required?
3. Modeling: The effective communicator models effective communication. According to Deanna Roberts, mentoring, whether as "coach, model, guide, teacher, sponsor, or advisor," is a valued skill.[38]
4. Checking for understanding: Is the receiver understanding the message? Is there an indication by nonverbal body signals that something is unclear?
5. Guided and independent practice: Is there an opportunity to practice communication, to act on the message that produces results? Are receivers encouraged to rely on past, present, (and future) experience?

Many of Hunter's concepts are similar to Tom Peters' concept of "Coaching"—those leaders who "encourage, excite, teach, listen, facilitate"—concepts so brilliantly articulated in his book *A Passion for Excellence*.[39]

Hunter is quick to point out that teaching is an art and a science (and we do study library *science*, do we not?). Some people "have a knack" for making communication an art. Library leaders must believe that everyone on the library staff is capable of effective communications. Most of all, more time should be devoted to checking for understanding; that is, taking the time to digest, question, reexamine, and summarize material that is used. In this way, honest, frequent feedback is provided. This avoids an elliptical language such as that expressed by the March Hare and Alice in Carroll's *Alice's Adventures in Wonderland*:

"Then you should say what you mean," the March Hare went on. "I do," Alice hastily replied; "at least—at least I mean what I say—that's the same thing, you know."

Making one's meaning clear and precise is an essential skill in effective communication.

Communicating about Library Leadership: The Third Wave

Peter Drucker has written about events that have caused dislocation and have created discontinuity over the past decade and that make this a turbulent time for decision makers (and, therefore, communicators).[40] John Berry has lamented, when several top posts in libraries were filled by people not in the library field, about the inability of librarianship to communicate "what a librarian is and does."[41] Effective communication is responsiveness and responsibility. Library leaders must offer a library language that addresses market awareness, flexibility, inspiration, and proactive communication skills, and provides the power to build meaningful connections through library networking. They must understand that leadership and communication have strong links to creativity. As Oscar Handlin points out, "Libraries . . . no longer hold a monopoly on information; a flourishing industry now makes such data available through numerous alternative channels."[42]

That is why to succeed in conveying the library's true mission, library leaders must speak not only eloquently, but effectively for library values. Personal and professional growth in library leadership communication consists of more than a series of memos, a plethora of committee meetings, or a batch of directives. In short, growing to greatness as a library communicator is a never-ending process.

References

1. Ron Smith, "Communication Skills: Key Ingredients for Success," *Millionaire* (March 1988): 34.
2. Herbert S. White, *Library Personnel Management* (White Plains, N.Y.: Knowledge Industry Publications, 1985), 149.
3. Barbara McEvoy, "Everybody Acts: How Principals Influence Development of Their Staffs," *Educational Leadership* (February 1987): 73–77.

4. Kenneth H. Blanchard, "Situational Leadership," *Principal* (March 1987): 12–16.
5. Clayton Sherman, "Coping with Pain-in-the-Neck Employees," *U.S. News & World Report* (December 14, 1987): 74.
6. Ron Zemke, "Empowerment: Helping People Take Charge," *Training* (January 1988): 63–64.
7. Donald M. Kendell, "The Four Simple Truths of Management: Bridges of Communication," *Vital Speeches of the Day* (May 15, 1986): 475–78.
8. Herbert S. White, "Oh, Where Have All the Leaders Gone?" *Library Journal* (October 1, 1987): 68–69.
9. U.S. Department of Education, *Alliance for Excellence: Librarians Respond to A Nation at Risk* (Washington, D.C.: U.S. Government Printing Office, 1984).
10. Marilyn L. Miller, "Statement . . . Before the Subcommittee on Education, Art, and Humanities, Senate Labor and Human Resources Committee on Reauthorization of Chapter 2, Education Consolidation and Improvement Act, July 16, 1987," *School Library Media Quarterly* (Winter 1988): 122–26.
11. Robert S. Alvarez, ed., "What's a Good Boss?" *Library Administrator's Digest* (February 1986): 14.
12. John Heider, *The Tao of Leadership* (Atlanta: Humanities New Age, 1985), 14.
13. Peter Drucker, *The Effective Executive* (New York: Harper & Row, 1967), 100.
14. "Marginalia," *The Chronicle of Higher Education* (February 24, 1988): A2.
15. Susan E. Russ, "A Bureaucrat's Guide to Chocolate Chip Cookies," *Washington Post* (February 4, 1987): 5. [Reprinted as a handout.]
16. Ron Smith, "Communication Skills: Key Ingredients for Success," *Millionaire* (March 1988): 35.
17. White, "Leaders," 149.
18. Robert Half, *How to Get Your Employees to Do What They're Supposed to Do* (New York: Robert Hall, 1984), 1–16.
19. Ibid., 13.
20. Norman D. Stevens, "Humor and Creativity," *College & Research Libraries News* 49 (March 1988): 145–46.
21. Margaret E. Galloway, "Introducing Junior Staff to the Administrative Process," *College & Research Libraries News* 48 (December 1987): 687–88.
22. Jan Keene, "The Equal Distribution of Dissatisfaction," *Library Administration & Management* (January 1988): 32–35.

23. Rosabeth Moss Kanter, *The Change Masters: Innovation for Productivity in the American Corporation* (New York: Simon & Schuster, 1983), 101–2.
24. White, "Leaders," 151.
25. Jay E. Daily, *Staff Personality Problems in the Library Automation Process* (Littleton, Colo.: Libraries Unlimited, 1985), 4.
26. Cheryl A. Price, "What Professional Librarians Expect from Administrators: One Librarian's View," *College & Research Libraries* 48 (September 1987): 408–12.
27. Deborah Fink, " . . . Another Librarian's View," *College & Research Libraries* 48 (September 1987): 413–17.
28. Brian Alley, " . . . An Administrator's Response," *College & Research Libraries* 48 (September 1987): 418–21.
29. "Business Bulletin," *The Wall Street Journal* (December 22, 1987): 1.
30. Stuart M. Schmidt and David Kipnis, "The Perils of Persistence," *Psychology Today* (November 1987): 32–34.
31. Clemens P. Work et al., "The 21st Century Executive," *U.S. News & World Report* (March 7, 1988): 48–56.
32. Peter Drucker, *The Effective Executive* (New York: Harper & Row, 1967), 25.
33. Jonathan A. Lindsey, ed., *Performance Evaluation: A Management Basic for Librarians* (Phoenix: The Oryx Press, 1986), vii.
34. Kenneth H. Blanchard, "Praise and Criticism: Finding the Right Ratio," *Today's Office* (December 1987): 14–16.
35. Sheila D. Creth, *Effective On-the-Job Training: Developing Library Human Resources* (Chicago: The American Library Association, 1986), 63.
36. Joseph A. Ruef, "The Pros and Cons of Management by Objectives," *Library Administration & Management* (January 1988): 40–41.
37. Madeline Hunter, "Staff Meetings That Produce Staff Development," *Principal* (January 1988): 44–45.
38. Deanna L. Roberts, "Mentoring in the Academic Library," *College & Research Libraries News* 47 (February 1986): 117–19.
39. Tom Peters and Nancy Austin, *A Passion for Excellence* (New York: Random House, 1985), 324.
40. Peter Drucker, *Managing in Turbulent Times* (New York: Harper & Row, 1980).
41. John Berry, "The Unknown Librarian," *Library Journal* (May 15, 1987): 4.
42. Oscar Handlin, "Libraries and Learning," *American Scholar* (Summer 1987): 205–18.

6

The Importance of Effective Communication to Library Leadership; or, Communication, Communication, Communication

SUSAN STEWART

If, as library professionals, our primary goal is to satisfy the informational requirements of our users, we may need to develop better strategies to fulfill those requirements. The rate of change in society and technology and the competition for ever dwindling resources, such as funds and quality personnel, make the need for developing more successful strategies critical. Library professionals, as professionals in all facets of society today, are becoming aware that being a good manager may not be enough. There has been a call for more sophisticated leadership skills. To achieve this, we need to go back to the basics of leadership: To paraphrase a familiar phrase from real estate the three most important factors in effective library leadership are: (1) communication, (2) communication, and (3) communication.

My experience with the power of communication and library leadership was formulated when I began library school at the University of Denver in 1983. *Megatrends* and *In Search of Excellence* had just been published, and one of my most dynamic professors, Anne Mathews, was putting the finishing touches on her book *Communicate!* There was also a rumor that the Rutgers Library School was to be merged with their School of Communications. This seemed to be the genesis of how librarianship was going to meet the challenges of the escalating number of changes being felt in the profession, the society, and the technology. If effective communication skills were what librarians or information specialists were all about, we already had the key to successfully meeting these new challenges.

Communication skills seemed to be used everywhere—assessing user needs for collection development, executing a thorough reference interview, informing funding sources of our needs, carrying out daily interactions between members of the library staff, setting meaningful performance goals for individual library staff members, working with vendors to fill various needs, and working with media to inform the public of our library's services. Everything seemed to be based on effective communication skills. Librarians already possessed the necessary foundation for effective leadership.

If we have this foundation, how can we enhance it to meet the changing needs of librarianship today? I will review the literature on the subject of leadership and develop a set of leadership characteristics, give a brief overview of the process of communication, underscore the vital connection between leadership and effective communications, and, finally, propose practical methods to assist librarians—from first-line supervisors to library directors—in becoming more effective in achieving the leadership necessary to carry our profession to ever-greater levels of success.

Leadership

My first experience with the concept of leadership was when I was about ten years old and had gone to a summer camp. I was extremely interested in the nature programs and the fellowship offered. At the end of the week, I was among a small group of campers chosen by the camp counselors to come back the next week for a "leadership" session. I was thrilled, yet confused, because my peers had also voted me the "most neat[tidy]" person in camp.

Upon reflection, I can see there were many keys that could be gleaned from that experience that are appropriate to our discussion. Just as effective communication, the concept of leadership seems to require at least two people or a group interacting with one another. The confirmation of the status was given by consensus of the group, based on the group's values. The camp counselors evidently felt neatness and interest in the concepts being taught were important. I must have been able to communicate those behaviors to the counselors and my fellow campers. The special session was to cost extra in both time and money. Another important facet of leadership behavior—like other behaviors—is choice. We have control over the choices and our behavior. If we desire to achieve effective leadership, we can improve our behavior patterns and attain it.

Leadership seems to be the central interest of all professionals, be they librarians, nurses, corporation officers, politicians, or military personnel. And now every form of media seems to be seeking this all-encompassing goal. If the 1960s were the "love generation," then the 1990s must be the "leadership generation." Is leadership the answer to all our hopes and dreams? How do other theorists define leadership?

G. Edward Evans states that "A person is assumed to have taken on a leadership role when that person exercises influence over a group, including directing group activities toward a goal."[1]

The term leadership is difficult to define, possibly because of the many personal experiences each individual brings to the concept. Historically, theories of leadership centered around various uncontrollable factors such as genetics and timing. Early theorists believed in what is generally called the "Great Man" theory. This meant that either you were a born leader or you were not. The next informal theory regarding leadership was that if you were not born into it, leadership was thrust upon you as a matter of circumstance, or as Warren G. Bennis and Burt Nanus state, "Great events made leaders of otherwise ordinary people."[2] This is similar to the idea that "timing is everything"; if you were in the right spot at the right time, you might be the next great leader.

In 1967, Fred E. Fiedler did some of the grass roots research on leadership. He described leadership behavior as "the particular acts in which a leader engages in the course of directing and coordinating the work of his group members."[3] Fiedler's "Contingency Model" theory postulated that "leadership effectiveness depends upon the appropriate matching of the individual's leadership style of interacting and the influence which the group situation provides."[4] In other words, the success of a leader is contingent on both the person's personal characteristics and the situation.

Next, political scientist James MacGregor Burns proposed two levels of leadership. "Transactional" leadership was primarily concerned with the actions necessary to carry on the daily routine of a business, while "transformational" leadership transformed the persons involved from the routine and motivated them to greater heights of production and self-fulfillment. More specifically, he stated that transformational leadership "occurs when one or more persons *engage* with others in such a way that leaders and followers raise one another to higher levels of motivation and morality. Their purposes, which might have started out separate but related, in the case of transactional leadership, become fused."[5]

Burns's theory was the basis of a recent research project by Bennis and Nanus, who interviewed and observed some ninety leaders from such varied backgrounds as business, academics, the arts, sports, and various social rights movements. Their research led them to this definition of leaders: "Managers do things right, leaders do the right thing."[6]

Bennis and Nanus proposed four strategies for becoming a leader:

Strategy I: Attention through Vision
An overpowering goal or focus of their energy.

Strategy II: Meaning through Communication
Ability to create meaning and share their vision.

Strategy III: Trust through Positioning
Persistence and integrity build confidence.

Strategy IV: The Deployment of Self through Positive Self Regard
Self-knowledge and self-acceptance.[7]

George P. Barbour, Jr., and George A. Sipel at the Center for Excellence in Local Government in Palo Alto, California, suggest that there are also four leadership behaviors:

1. visioning
2. communicating your vision
3. acting on your vision
4. caring about people and the organization[8]

Robert Tannenbaum and Warren H. Schmidt offer a similar definition: "Successful leaders understand themselves, the people they are dealing with, and the company and broader social environment in which they operate."[9]

As stated previously, there are many definitions and characteristics of leadership: (1) a knowledge of self, the group, and the overall situation, (2) a compelling need or vision to improve the group and the situation, (3) an ability to communicate that vision in terms of the receiver of that message, and (4) an ability to adjust to feedback.

Communication

What about communication? Not only is leadership impossible without effective communication, but there are many similarities between leadership and effective communication skills. I would like to discuss briefly the process of communication; some types of communication (verbal, nonverbal, and written); and interference to the communication process.

In basic communication, a sender formulates a message, based on the sender's background, that is sent to a receiver. The message is sent by whatever means the sender chooses, usually verbal, nonverbal, or written.

The receiver receives the message and, based on the receiver's background and the perceived meanings of the symbols, accepts it. At that time the receiver gives the sender feedback about the message that may qualify or answer the sender's original message. If the communication is effective, the two will have shared meanings and understandings. The simplicity of this interpretation belies the sophistication that is required to actually make sure that the message that was sent was the one that was received. That is the whole key to effective communication. T. Harrell Allen states that "communication is simply sharing information with others. If it is effective it means shared meaning—shared understanding." [10] How do we achieve shared meaning and therefore shared understanding?

There are many factors that affect how the receiver will understand the message one sends. Such things as the individual's experience, abilities, culture, environment, focus of attention, and even such things as the time of day are some of the factors that may affect the communication process.

Verbal communications rely first on having a shared meaning for various sounds. If, for example, you are at the reference desk and a person calls in and only speaks Russian, and neither you nor your colleagues speak Russian, it is very unlikely that the two of you will effectively communicate.

On a more complex level, even when two people speak the same language the communications may not always have shared meanings for the symbols or sounds used. One person's experience with a word may be different from another's experience. For example, if your library has a videotape collection, is it VHS or BETA or both? This distinction will be important to the prospective library user.

The physical setting of where the communication takes place may also have an impact on the effectiveness of the communication. The communication exchange in a coffee break discussion will probably have a far different structure and less serious effect than one that takes place in the library director's office. The same may be true for the time of day. Some people are more alert at one time of the day than they are at another.

The preceding discussion has focused on the basics for relatively minimal verbal communication to take place. More recently, research has shown that nonverbal communication may be more credible and carry more weight than verbal exchanges. In fact, according to Allen, "Only seven percent of a message's effect is carried by words, and the listener receives the other 93 percent through nonverbal means." [11]

The importance of nonverbal communication has been studied more extensively in the past few decades. Facial expressions, "body language," "dressing for success," and the tone of a person's voice have all been explored to gain insight into what people are saying when they are not "saying" anything.

In terms of nonverbal communications in a library setting, what does your body language or facial expression communicate when the thirteenth person of the day asks, "Where is the *Readers' Guide?*" What about the atmosphere in your library? Is the building effectively lighted? Are surroundings pleasant and inviting? Is there enough parking for staff at peak user times? What about the temperature of your building? These are subtle means of nonverbal communications that speak to our users and staff about how important we believe both their needs, and ours, are.

Written communication is an almost exclusively one-way form of communication. It goes from the sender to the receiver with little or no means for immediate feedback or reinforcement. What do the signs in your building say to your users? How do you use written communication in your organization? Policies and procedures are essential in assisting staff to perform routine tasks, but the satisfaction of using only written memos as your chief method of communication to staff would not be conducive to effective communication. The inability to receive feedback or clarification of the message is lost on written communication. Thus, we have the basic process of communication, some examples of the various types of communication, and ways in which communications are influenced.

Communication and Leadership

Just how important is communication to leadership? Bennis and Nanus see it as "Strategy II" in the linking of a person's vision with those able to assist in the ability to produce that vision. Ernest L. Stech may have summed it up best when he articulated, "If communication is not all of the game of leadership, it is a big part." [12] In Thomas J. Peters and Robert H. Waterman, Jr.'s report of excellent companies, they reported that "the excellent companies are a vast network of informal, open communications." [13] Allen further affirms that "elements of leadership are of course all fused together through communication." [14] Communication seems to be almost taken for granted as a foundation for effective leadership.

It has been postulated that leadership and communication skills are behaviors and that behaviors are learned. Next, we need to choose to learn or relearn those skills. Leadership is not a panacea that will solve all the world's problems without effort. If you are truly committed to your personal goals, your staff goals, and the needs of the public, you will begin to see that enhancing communication skills will enhance your leadership abilities.

Practical Implications

The following summarizes change processes:

1. Awareness that current behaviors may not be effective in fulfilling needs or producing the desired results
2. Assessment of strengths and weaknesses
3. Review of alternatives
4. Commitment to making the necessary changes
5. Following through

How can we become more aware of the behaviors that are not fulfilling our needs and therefore must be changed? As Donald E. Riggs pointed out, "There is something seriously wrong when the most popular library workshops are stress management and planning for early retirement." [15] He further states that national organizations such as ALA should offer more workshops and continuing education classes in the area of leadership. I agree that these would help, but there are other strategies that would help more people if we became more aware of our own situation.

For many librarians, and far more library supervisors, the workshops that ALA offers, and will offer, are too far-removed from their reach in space and cost. We need to begin "in our own backyards." This is important because even though it is crucial that the library director be the leader, innovator, and goal setter for the library as a whole, research by Fiedler demonstrates that "the first-line supervisor plays an important role in determining group performance, group morale, and job satisfaction." [16] Leadership needs to be pervasive throughout the organization, not just at the top, to be effective.

So the question again is *how*. We need to go back to the basics and remember that change begins with each one of us. How long has it been since you did an assessment of yourself, your public, and your staff? How long has it been since you felt you really communicated with each of those three and reflected on what is needed to enhance goals and the needs of staff and public?

Formal interviews, questionnaires, or workshops are some formal assessment methods. Often, very important information is found in the most informal settings. For example, listening to how to behave in certain situations and how the staff interacts with each other and the public can offer insight into organization needs. The key is to listen sincerely, actively, and objectively.

How else are we able to use communication skills to enhance our leadership roles? Opportunity for communication is another method. If staff workshops on communication are not in the budget, how about some simple suggestion-box approaches for both staff and public? Other methods include: newsletters; weekly, monthly or annual question-and-answer periods; and evaluation sessions on where we are now and where we are going. Setting the tone for open communications to take place will go a long way toward improving the goals of the library. At our university library we have found that "brown bag" lunches on "hot" library issues are effective in promoting open communications. The realization that leaders cannot do everything and do not have all the answers can only be remedied by giving other people input into the process.

Another step in the effective use of communication to enhance leadership skills is feedback. By opening up the opportunity for communications and listening, two of the basic steps are taken. But to make sure the message was understood or that you understand the other person's message or response, you must request or present the necessary feedback. This may be done by restating what you believe the person was saying or by asking questions about the message.

Once you have made sure that the message received was the one that was sent, examine the alternatives for a solution to the situation. Usually there is a cost associated with each alternative, so the decision will have to take into account the costs and the benefits. Once a decision is arrived at, the leader and group must commit to the changes and follow through on them.

Conclusion

Effective leadership is based on (1) an awareness of self, the group, and the situation of that combination; (2) an assessment of the needs of the self and group—focusing on developing a vision toward fulfilling them; (3) the ability to communicate the vision in terms of the receivers; and (4) the ability to carry through and adjust to feedback.

We have the power to change and to succeed. As librarians, we are well schooled and can be nearly anything we want to be.

Through the preceding steps and the use of positive communication skills, we can take our position of leadership.

References

1. G. Edward Evans, *Management Techniques for Librarians* (New York: Academic Press, 1983), 119.

2. Warren G. Bennis and Burt Nanus, *Leaders: The Strategies for Taking Charge* (New York: Harper & Row, 1985), 5.
3. Fred E. Fiedler, *A Theory of Leadership Effectiveness* (New York: McGraw-Hill, 1967), 26.
4. Ibid., 347.
5. James MacGregor Burns, *Leadership* (New York: Harper & Row, 1978), 20.
6. Bennis and Nanus, *Leaders*, 21.
7. Ibid., 26–68.
8. George P. Barbour, Jr., and George A. Sipel, "Excellence in Leadership: Public Sector Model," *Public Management* 68 (August 1986): 3–5.
9. Robert Tannenbaum and Warren H. Schmidt, "How to Choose a Leadership Pattern," *Harvard Business Review* 36 (March–April 1968): 129.
10. T. Harrell Allen, *The Bottom Line: Communicating in the Organization* (Chicago: Nelson-Hall, 1979), 9.
11. Ibid., 18.
12. Ernest L. Stech, *Leadership Communication* (Chicago: Nelson-Hall, 1983), 9.
13. Thomas J. Peters and Robert H. Waterman, Jr., *In Search of Excellence, Lessons from America's Best-Run Companies* (New York: Harper & Row, 1982), 21–22.
14. Allen, *The Bottom Line*, 99.
15. Donald E. Riggs, "Leadership Is Imperative," *Technicalities* 5 (November 1985): 10.
16. Fiedler, *Leadership Effectiveness*, 236.

7

A Review of Leadership Research

EUGENE S. MITCHELL

> Probably more has been written and less known about leadership
> than any other topic in the behavioral sciences.
>
> Warren G. Bennis

One message comes through loud and clear to anyone who performs even a cursory review of the literature of leadership research: despite the large amount of research done, we still know very little about leadership.[1]

Nobel Prize winner James MacGregor Burns, in his book *Leadership*, published in 1978, described our lack of understanding in this way:

> We know far too little about *leadership*. We fail to grasp the essence
> of leadership that is relevant to the modern age and hence we cannot
> agree even on the standards by which to measure, recruit, and reject it.
> Is leadership merely innovation—cultural or political? Is it essentially
> inspiration? Mobilization of followers? Goal setting? Goal fulfillment?
> Is the leader the definer of values? Satisfier of needs? If leaders require
> followers, who leads whom from where to where, and why? How do
> leaders lead followers without being wholly led *by* followers? Leadership
> is one of the most observed and least understood phenomena on earth.[2]

This lack of understanding is also true in the field of librarianship. Andrea C. Dragon commented in her dissertation that "leadership, although recognized by management theorists as an element in the management process, is generally neglected in the literature of library administration. Little is known about the leader behavior pattern of library administrators."[3]

The reaction of the library profession has been, according to Joanne R. Euster, "some soul-searching, a wide variety of management workshops, courses and programs, a plethora of MLS/MBAs, and very little theory or research into what constitutes library leadership."[4]

The need for librarians to understand the complex phenomenon of leadership is of pressing concern. Fundamental changes affecting the future of the profession are going to require strong leaders to help achieve its goals. To the extent that librarians can understand some of the variables of the leadership function, we can perform better when we are called upon to lead.

The real problem is that no single best model of leadership effectiveness has emerged from almost a century of research—we have not been able to come up with *the* "Theory of Leadership" or with a list of "Ten Laws of Leadership." Leadership is a very difficult concept to study, and an integrated understanding of it still eludes us. The various theories that do exist merely provide frameworks for studying different aspects of the phenomenon. As such, however, they are still valuable.

An important first step in understanding the "language of leadership" is to understand the leadership research. This chapter will survey the history and development of some of the major theories and concepts of leadership.

Definition

One major obstacle is definitional. Ralph Melvin Stogdill presents eleven categories of definitions of leadership,[5] and Euster reduces them to five broad classes.[6] For purposes here, the definition of leadership in very general terms is "the process of influencing the activities of an individual or a group in efforts toward goal achievement in a given situation."[7]

Trait Approach

Discussions of leadership can be found in the writings of the ancient Chinese and Egyptians, but it was not until the early 1900s that scientific research into the topic began. The research at the beginning of this century first focused on the personality characteristics presumed to set leaders apart from others. This line of research was known as the "Great

Man" theory. Some of the characteristics that were identified and studied included physical factors (height, weight, age, appearance), fluency of speech, intelligence, self-confidence, emotional control, social and economic status, popularity, and prestige. Although some correlations were shown between these traits and effectiveness, this line of research did not prove to be very fruitful because the relationships discovered (although statistically significant) were weak and of limited predictive value. In addition, longitudinal comparisons of effective and ineffective leaders in identical or similar roles were not conducted. Instead, the methodology used was to compare the traits of leaders with the traits of followers. Finally, too many inconsistencies and contradictions appeared as researchers tried to develop a universal theory of leadership. Some of the same traits were found in both leaders and followers.

New Concepts

As interest in the trait approach waned, research branched out to include the study of situational variables, leader behavior (as opposed to traits), organizational outcomes, and environmental variables that seemed to affect the organizational outcomes of leadership. The interaction of certain personality attributes of the leader and characteristics of the particular situation—call them situational variables—result in leader behaviors that help determine organizational outcomes. In other words, situational variables and personal attributes of the leader relate to organizational outcomes only through the leader's behavior—what the leader does. To make the picture complete, of course, we would need to consider certain environmental variables such as economic conditions, laws, and interest groups that also influence organizational outcomes. Consequently, researchers became interested in learning what specific things leaders do (that is, behaviors) to make them effective in organizations. They wanted to know to what extent we can predict these behaviors by knowing something about leader attributes and the situations in which leaders find themselves.

Leader Behavior

By the early 1950s, researchers started becoming disenchanted with the trait approach and began to study leader behavior, that is, what leaders actually *do*. A wide variety of activities in which leaders engage were identified and researchers tried to group them together. Two similar results were developed independently at Ohio State University and the University of Michigan.

At Ohio State, two major dimensions were identified by Edwin A. Fleishman and Ralph Melvin Stogdill: consideration and initiation of structure.[8] Consideration referred to "the extent to which a leader exhibited concern for the welfare of the other members of the group"; initiation of structure referred to "the extent to which a leader initiated activity in the group, organized it, and defined the way the work was to be done." To measure these two factors, the researchers developed the Leadership Behavior Description Questionnaire (LBDQ) in which subordinates were asked to describe the behavior of their supervisors.

The results of the Ohio State studies were mixed. However, leaders were generally rated more effective when they scored high in both consideration and initiating structure. The greatest effectiveness was usually achieved when a combination of both factors was present, the actual mix of the two being influenced by situational variables.

Robert R. Blake and Jane H. Mouton attempted to apply the results of the Ohio State research in the development of their prescriptive model called the "managerial grid."[9] They suggested that the single most effective leadership style would be a "team" approach (high consideration, high initiating structure). The least desirable leadership style would be characterized by low consideration and low initiating structure.

The managerial grid made intuitive sense because it was simple and suggested the "best way" to lead. The problem is that no leader can realistically be expected to be *both* considerate and structure initiating in *every* task. The weakness of the managerial grid was that it did not consider the variables that could distinguish one situation from another.

At the University of Michigan, Rensis Likert also identified two dimensions in effective leader behavior that he distinguished as job centered and employee centered.[10] His studies suggested that both sets of behavior improve performance, but that employee-centered behaviors led to better group morale.

In applying the results of his research, Likert postulated four systems of management: exploitive-authoritative, benevolent-authoritative, consultative, and participative-group. Although he found that most organizations existed in an environment between benevolent-authoritative and consultative, he believed that the most effective leader behavior would be participative-group. By suggesting the best way to lead a group, this model (like the managerial grid) failed to account for the situational variables that must be considered in determining leadership effectiveness.

Situational Variables

By the 1970s, the important role played by situational variables in predicting organizational outcomes was realized and led to a situational approach in the study of research. A few of the most prominent approaches are described here.

One of the earliest discussions of the situational and contingent nature of leadership was led by Robert Tannenbaum and Warren H. Schmidt and has come to be referred to as the "leadership continuum." [11] In their view, leadership comprised seven styles ranging from highly boss centered to highly subordinate centered, depending on the amount of authority granted to the subordinates by the leader. The amount of authority granted depended on forces operating in the leader's personality, forces in the subordinates, and forces in the situation.

While not supported by research studies, this model was still important because it was an early attempt to conceptualize the idea that the appropriate leadership style depended on situational variables and personalities. The model suggested a variety of styles, not a best one. The model was also used to describe the value of participation by subordinates in the decision-making process.

The "situational leadership theory," developed by Paul Hersey and Kenneth H. Blanchard, considers the maturity of the group being led. [12] It was originally called the "life cycle theory of leadership" and is based on the observation that people, in this case subordinates, change and mature as they gain knowledge and experience. According to the theory, the maturity of the group must be considered in deciding on the appropriate leader behavior. In other words, leader behaviors must be geared toward the needs of the subordinates in a given situation. The behaviors prescribed by this theory are based on the consideration and initiation of structure dimensions of the Ohio State studies, but here the dimensions are called relationship and task behaviors.

Group maturity is introduced as the situational variable and is divided into two parts: job maturity (the group member's ability to do the job) and psychological maturity (the group member's willingness to do the job). Group maturity is measured by appropriate scales, and subordinates are classified as either high or low in both job and psychological maturity. As a result, four levels of maturity are identified: low (low ability, low willingness), moderately low (low ability, high willingness), moderately high (high ability, low willingness) and high (high ability, high willingness).

As a result, Hersey and Blanchard developed a model that suggests that, as the group maturity changes, the leader should adjust the balance between task and relationship behaviors accordingly. A low-maturity situation requires high-task and low-relationship behaviors, whereas the leader of a high-maturity group can delegate more and be less engaged in either task or relationship activities.

The "vertical dyad linkage theory" developed by Gordon Graen and his associates concentrates on the formation of relationships between leaders and individual subordinates. [13] This theory holds that effective leader behaviors directed toward individual subordinates depend on the relationship established between the leader and each subordinate.

A vertical dyad is a superior-subordinate pairing. Each dyad can fall into one of three categories: an in group, an out group, and a middle group. The nature of the dyad coupled with the leader behavior exhibited creates three patterns of exchange called "linkages." An in-group relationship is usually an open, high-quality one. The dyad linkage involves leadership on the part of the superior, characterized by two-way communication, shared decision making, mutual support and trust, and freedom. The second type of linkage, found in low-quality, out-group relationships, is characterized by supervision rather than leadership. The relationship is more formal with essentially downward communication. The leader engages in more task-oriented, structuring behaviors. The subordinate accepts legitimate authority in exchange for pay and benefits. The middle group linkage is characterized as stewardship in a basically noncommittal relationship. Two-way communication most often resembles negotiation and the leader engages in task-oriented behaviors.

The theory predicts that where the vertical dyad linkage is of the in-group type, job performance will be better, job satisfaction will be higher, and there will be fewer problems with supervision.

The "contingency model of leadership effectiveness" developed by Fred E. Fiedler proposes an interaction between leader style and the favorableness of the situation for the leader. [14]

Fiedler contends that a group's effectiveness is contingent upon the appropriate match between leadership style and the degree to which the leader has control and influence over the situation. There are two basic leadership styles: task motivated and relationship motivated. A task-motivated leadership style meets the leader's need to gain satisfaction from performing the task; a relationship-motivated leadership style is oriented toward achieving good interpersonal relations within the work group and satisfies the leader's need to gain a position of prominence.

Situational control is the moderating variable in the relationship between leadership style and effective performance. It refers to the degree to which the dimensions of the group situation give the leader power and influence over the group. Fiedler's model considers three situational dimensions confronting the leader. In order of importance, they are leader-member relations, task structure, and position power. The particular mix of these three variables determines situational control.

These variables are dichotomized to provide eight categories of situations ranging from highly favorable to highly unfavorable for the leader. Task-motivated leaders perform best in situations that are highly favorable or in those that are highly unfavorable. Relationship-oriented leaders tend to perform best in situations that have moderate favorableness.

The "path-goal theory" developed by Robert J. House suggests means by which the leader can identify paths to convergent organizational and individual goals.[15] It assumes that an individual can adopt different behavior patterns depending on the needs of the situation at any point in time. It is based on an assumption commonly found in leadership research that leader behavior affects organizational outcomes only to the extent that this behavior influences subordinates to do something in support of organization goals. The leader is then forced to consider the characteristics of the subordinate as situational variables and tries to add to or subtract from the existing potential of the subordinates. Subordinate characteristics are divided into two categories: those that relate to the subordinates themselves (their needs, abilities, locus of control) and those that relate to the work environment (nature of the task, group, norms and maturity, and nature of the formal authority system).

Leader behaviors, in turn, are divided into four types derived from the consideration and initiating structure categories: instrumental, participative, supportive, and achievement-oriented. As suggested above, the leader must decide which behavior is appropriate given the nature of the situation (i.e., the characteristics of the subordinates). The correct match will result in subordinate satisfaction, improved performance, increased effort, and higher motivation.

Library Leadership Research

As suggested at the beginning of this chapter, there has been little leadership research done in the area of librarianship. A review of *Comprehensive Dissertation Abstracts* revealed a few dissertations on the topic.

Several researchers used the Leadership Behavior Description Questionnaire to determine and examine perceptions and expectations of leadership behavior. Michael B. Binder tested the applicability of organizational situational theory to the supervision of technical services, specifically cataloging and processing, in large academic libraries.[16] He found that little, if any, relationship existed between three situational factors (the kind of work supervised, the educational level of the work group supervised, and the supervisory level) and the supervisory behavior of cataloging and processing personnel as measured through their self-perceptions and self-expectations.

James F. Comes investigated the influence that academic library directors have on goal setting and goal achievement.[17] He found no correlation between either the middle-management perception of leader behavior of the directors and the existence of selected goals as perceived by middle-management supervisors; or the middle-management perceptions of leader behavior of the directors and the level of goal achievement as perceived by middle-management supervisors. A significant difference was found between middle management's perceptions of the director's leader behavior and the director's self-perceptions of leader behavior.

Andrea Dragon, Galen E. Rike, and Rita Sparks investigated and described the discrepancy between leader-behavior descriptions made by library administrators and their subordinates.[18] Dragon found that a discrepancy existed between library administrators' self-description of their behavior and that behavior as described by their subordinate group. Rike determined that the agreement on expectations for the staff-leadership role of directors of state library agencies is greater than the agreement on perceptions of the behavior of the directors. Sparks, examining the library of one state university, showed a close correlation between leader and subordinate perception of the leader with respect to initiating structure but not with respect to consideration.

Dock A. Boyd assessed the relationship between the organizational characteristics of complexity and centralization and the rate of change in public libraries.[19] With respect to leadership, he found (among other things) little perceived relationship between leadership style and rate of change; the more formalized the library, the more likely its leadership style will be structurally oriented. Libraries that have a high degree of authority are more structurally oriented.

Edwin M. Cortez examined the effects of library directors' theories of management upon middle managers' managerial behavior and middle managers' job satisfaction in medium-sized public libraries.[20] His investigation showed that no direct or significant relationship existed between directors' management theories and middle managers' behavior or job satisfaction.

I have tested the validity of Fiedler's contingency model for predicting the effectiveness of academic library department heads. While my results showed that different types of situational control do exist in academic library departments, little support was found for the model in other areas. There was no relationship between leader motivation and leadership effectiveness under different conditions of situational control, that is, task-motivated leaders were no more or less effective than relationship-motivated leaders in highly favorable situations. Task structure and position power were found to account for the most variance in effectiveness.

Summary

This review of the major approaches to the study of leadership and their extensions into librarianship reveals that there is still no generally accepted one. As theories and models are developed, they merely add new dimensions to be studied. Research must and does continue.

The main purpose and value in providing this review is to provide library leaders, both actual and potential, with a basic theoretical understanding so that they might develop the skills required to understand and deal with the many factors involved in the leadership process.

Stogdill has suggested that as we look at the future of leadership research, we must keep in mind that research will reflect society.[21] As we shift from a manufacturing to a service economy, effective human relationships and personnel skills will become even more important. This will be true in librarianship as well. Donald E. Riggs warned that societal changes affecting libraries (such as the inflationary erosion of book budgets, shrinkage of staff size, and the abbreviation of services) will require more effective leadership. "Leaders, not managers, will advance our libraries through the 1980s and 90s into the year 2000."[22] It is hoped that this review will help to prepare us librarians for the assumption of this leadership role.

References

1. Warren G. Bennis, "Leadership Theory and Administrative Behavior: The Problems of Authority," *Administrative Science Quarterly* 4 (1959): 259–301.
2. James MacGregor Burns, *Leadership* (New York: Harper & Row, 1978), 5.
3. Andrea C. Dragon, "Self-descriptions and Subordinate Descriptions of the Leader Behavior of Library Administrators," *Dissertation Abstracts International* 37 (1976): 7380A–7381A.
4. Joanne R. Euster, "Leaders and Managers; Literature Review, Synthesis and a New Conceptual Framework," *Journal of Library Administration* 5 (1984): 45.
5. Ralph Melvin Stogdill, *Stogdill's Handbook of Leadership* (New York: Free Press, 1981).
6. Euster, "Leaders and Managers," 45.
7. Paul Hersey and Kenneth H. Blanchard, *Management of Organizational Behavior*, 3d ed. (Englewood Cliffs, N.J.: Prentice-Hall, 1977).
8. Edwin A. Fleishman, "Twenty Years of Consideration and Structure,"

in *Current Developments in the Study of Leadership*, eds. Edwin A. Fleishman and James G. Hunt (Carbondale, Ill.: Southern Illinois University Press, 1973), 1–40; Stogdill, *Stogdill's Handbook*.

9. Robert R. Blake and Jane H. Mouton, *The Managerial Grid* (Houston: Gulf Publishing Co., 1964).
10. Rensis Likert, *New Patterns of Management* (New York: McGraw-Hill, 1961).
11. Robert Tannenbaum and Warren H. Schmidt, "How to Choose a Leadership Pattern," *Harvard Business Review* 36 (October 1958): 96–101.
12. Hersey and Blanchard, *Management*.
13. Gordon Graen and James F. Cashman, "A Role-making Model of Leadership in Formal Organizations: A Developmental Approach," in *Leadership Frontier*, eds. James G. Hunt and Lars L. Larson (Kent, Ohio: Kent State University Press, 1975), 143–65.
14. Fred E. Fiedler, *A Theory of Leadership Effectiveness* (New York: McGraw-Hill, 1967).
15. Robert J. House, "A Path-Goal Theory of Leader Effectiveness," *Administrative Science Quarterly* 16 (1971): 321–38.
16. Michael B. Binder, "The Supervisory Behavior of Academic Library Cataloging and Processing Personnel: An Inquiry into Relationships with Certain Situational Factors," *Dissertation Abstracts International* 34 (1973): 3443A.
17. James F. Comes, "Relationships between Leadership Behavior and Goal Attainment in Selected Academic Libraries," *Dissertation Abstracts International* 39 (1978): 5782A.
18. Dragon, "Self-descriptions and Subordinate Descriptions"; Galen E. Rike, "Staff Leadership Behavior of Directors of State Library Agencies: A Study of Role Expectations and Perceived Fulfillment," *Dissertation Abstracts International* 37 (1976): 7382A–7383A; Rita Sparks, "Library Management: Consideration and Structure," *Journal of Academic Librarianship* 2 (1976): 66–71.
19. Dock A. Boyd, "Leadership, Organizational Dynamics and Rate of Change in Selected Public Libraries in the Northeastern United States," *Dissertation Abstracts International* 41 (1979): 1261A–1262A.
20. Edwin M. Cortez, "The Effects of Library Directors' Theory of Management upon Middle Management Behavior in Medium-size Public Libraries," *Dissertation Abstracts International* 41 (1980): 1262A.
21. Stogdill, *Stogdill's Handbook*, 34.
22. Donald E. Riggs, "Leadership Is Imperative," *Technicalities* 5 (November 1985): 9–11.

Part 2

Psychological Factors

Words are poor conveyors of meaning—in fact, it is a wonder that two people ever do understand each other.

Carl Rogers

Communication, like leadership, is a phenomenon that is much talked about, but is not understood very well. This section addresses some of the more difficult areas of communication (e.g., empathy, feedback, mediation).

Leadership is often described as a form of persuasion, through communication, to inspire and lead constituents or followers toward achievement of group goals. Leaders must understand the mutual dependence between individual and group and must understand that our tradition requires the balancing of the two. The mutual dependence between individual and group is ancient. But today if our communities are to survive, and if we are to survive as social beings, we must alter somewhat the nature of the relationship. Historically, the society supplied most of the continuity and coherence through its long-established belief systems and nurturing institutions. In return the individual gave allegiance, but except in time of war it was rather passive allegiance. Individuals accepted their culture as infants accept their cradle. It was the nurturing environment that enveloped them.[1]

Obviously any attempt to understand the leader-constituent relationship takes us onto psychological ground, and this is a good time to comment on psychoanalytic interpretations of leadership and communication. Much silliness has been perpetrated by shallow diagnoses of leaders based on one or another school of psychoanalysis. Even when Freud wrote of leadership he tended to see it so exclusively through his own theoretical lens that much of the rich complexity of the subject was filtered out. It would be a serious mistake, however, to reject psychoanalytic ideas, or "psycho-history" in general. Freud's thinking has made important contributions to our understanding of all human behavior, including leadership.[2]

Communication is an idea transplant. The center fielder may have the right idea about who should catch the fly ball, but unless the center fielder can transplant his or her ideas into the minds of his or her teammates, the center fielder may be through in baseball. Almost every area of human endeavor revolves around the efforts of people to get ideas into the minds of their peers, and the leadership of libraries is no exception. To make the idea transplant as successful as possible, the library leader should endeavor to develop a continuing awareness of the basic process of encoding-sending-receiving-decoding and the natural pitfalls of each step in the communication process.

An old psychologist joke shows one counselor meeting another on an elevator and saying, "You're O.K., how am I?" As library leaders analyze their communication activities, they should keep in mind their various ego states and the impact these have on interpersonal relationships.

The best way to appraise the quality of a library leader is to look at the leader's followers. What kind of followers are they? How strong is their commitment? Are they reaching the library's goals? If the library's goals are wisely chosen and efficiently reached, then one can assume that sound leadership practices are in place. However, one must also be concerned about long-term goal design and achievement. Mutual goal design and achievement can be best realized through a short- and long-range planning process. The library leader, with the library department heads, creates a strategic vision that is communicated throughout the library construct. To support the vision (mission) statement, broad goals and specific objectives are carefully crafted, followed by the formulation of strategies (courses of action) for achieving the goals and objectives. Library leadership essentially operates on a continuum theory of personality. It suggests that the types of leadership attitudes toward subordinates may be accurately charted along a continuum. At one end of the system would be the total authoritarian. The benevolent autocrat would fall somewhere near the middle. At the other end of the line are the democratic-laissez-faire leaders. One interpretation of the continuum theory is that the two extremes represent opposite centers of concern—the authoritarian leader being job centered and the democratic leader being people or employee centered.[3] The democratic library leader will be more tolerant and emphathetic in dealing with others, providing feedback to complete the communication circle, and resolving conflict between or among library employees.

There are many concepts drawn from psychology and psychoanalysis that can be useful to the library leader and the student of leadership. In the most memorable conversations the rational, verbal, conscious elements of the exchange are supplemented by communication at another level—nonrational, nonverbal, and unconscious. Words and sentences, tone of voice, body language, facial expression, timing, unfinished sentences, silences—all contribute to a multilevel dialogue. And so it is in the continuing communication complexities between leaders and followers.[4] Successful library leaders usually have a good to excellent understanding of the human psyche. Effective communication with the complex human mind should never be perceived as an easy task. Furthermore, the intricacies of the endeavor become even greater in the leader-follower environment. The democratic leader understands and respects the follower and does what is necessary to manage the psychological nuances involved in the communication process.

References

1. John W. Gardner, *The Moral Aspect of Leadership* (Washington, D.C.: Independent Sector, 1987), 13.
2. John W. Gardner, *The Heart of the Matter: Leader-Constituent Interaction* (Washington, D.C.: Independent Sector, 1986), 10.
3. Robert M. Fulmer, *The New Management* (New York: Macmillan, 1974), 326.
4. Gardner, *The Heart of the Matter*, 11.

8

The Roll of Empathy in Managerial Communication

PEGGY JOHNSON

Two assumptions about communication are widely held by most managers: we spend significant amounts of our time communicating, and, if we do it well, we will progress up the career ladder. Researchers have confirmed both of these assumptions. Studies estimate the amount of time a manager spends communicating at 50 to 90 percent. Such well-respected authors as Peter Drucker, Henry Mintzberg, and Leonard R. Sayles have explored this area.[1] Research has shown that career advancement does indeed depend on the ability to communicate well. Various surveys verify this conclusion, including those by the *Harvard Business Review* and *Fortune*.[2] Clearly, if we desire to be effective and successful library managers, we need to develop our communication skills.

An operational definition of communication is the transmission of messages back and forth, person to person. Communication involves a transaction between people; it may be written, verbal, or nonverbal. The objective of communication is the sharing of meaning or understanding between two or more persons. The objective of organizational communication is sending and receiving information that serves the purposes of the organization. Communication is a constant of the human condition. As Paul Watzlawick has pointed out, you cannot *not* communicate.[3] It is the responsibility of a manager to do it well and, further, to facilitate effective communication throughout the organization.

William S. Howell feels that the most successful communication is based on empathy, resulting in the ability to respond quickly and appropriately to another person in an interchange.[4] According to Howell, an exceptionally able communicator is distinguished from a person with average skills by a greater facility in coping with the unexpected. An individual who can intuitively share another's perception of and response to a message is in a better position to direct, motivate, lead, instruct, persuade, and all the other tasks a manager needs to accomplish through communication. A competent manager practices continuous feedback in an effort to share understanding.

This chapter will expand on the role of communication, trust, openness, empathy, and intuition as attributes of effective communicators, and the responsibility of library managers to foster a communication climate manifesting these attributes.

Communication in the Organizational Setting

As far back as 1938, Chester I. Barnard identified the main task of an executive as communication.[5] A number of studies over the years have measured the time spent on communication activities. Sayles determined that 50 to 80 percent of a first-line supervisor's time is spent in direct, face-to-face contact with people.[6] Mintzberg examined the five media that managers have at their command—documents, telephone calls, scheduled and unscheduled meetings, and observational tours. He concluded that managers strongly favor the verbal media. His studies show managers spend 66 to 80 percent of their time in verbal communication, confirming Sayles's earlier research.[7] David Kenneth Berlo observed that more than 70 percent of the average person's time goes into listening, speaking, reading, and writing.[8]

Clearly, every person in an organization spends the majority of his or her time seeing, receiving, originating, transmitting, storing, recalling, misplacing, and forgetting information.[9] Misunderstanding information must be appended to this list. Studies have shown that people misunderstand or misinterpret 75 percent of what they hear.[10] Successfully bridging this "gap of misunderstanding" is a manager's responsibility.[11] The need for a manager to have effective communication skills is so widely articulated that it is nearly a cliché in management literature. Nevertheless, the need is real.

A *Harvard Business Review* study in 1964 examined the prevailing image among business people of the individual who should and does get ahead. The ability to communicate was chosen by more than 90 percent of the respondents as one of the nine most important factors in promotion.[12] Rudi Klauss and Bernard M. Bass describe managerial communication as "one of the most critical areas of organizational communication in general and . . . the point at which managerial behavior can genuinely make a difference in influencing performance and employee attitudes."[13] Effective library managers also realize that their success depends on effective communication skills. Not only is it the responsibility of a library manager to communicate well, it is also his or her responsibility to facilitate effective communication throughout the organization.

There are several barriers to effective organizational communication. They range from failure to share information appropriately (or at all) to information overload. In theory, these types of problems can be overcome by understanding who needs what types of information and when. A much more pervasive obstacle to effective communication is that which differentiates one individual from another—that is, each person's unique and personal experience and how it defines his or her perception of reality. This chapter will investigate ways to improve communication across this barrier.

Modern work organizations are frequently large and incredibly complex. They are characterized by interdependent relationships among highly diverse groups of people. Library organizations follow these trends. Libraries are generally a mixture of highly specialized professionals, paraprofessionals, clerical employees, and, often, part-time staff. An automation librarian who speaks only in computer jargon may not be able to explain to a public services librarian why a particular element of a record is not displaying in the on-line catalog. Library managers who fail to appreciate the complexity of the social milieu inside their organizations will underestimate the difficulties of being effective, efficient, and responsible leaders.[14] It is the complexities of interpersonal experience and relationships that complicate interpersonal communication.

Since perception, experience, background, and behavior vary from individual to individual, communication is a highly personal process. Leaders must consciously move beyond the personal barriers that lead to misunderstanding. They need to communicate more effectively by fostering a positive organizational environment for communication. R. Wayne Pace and Robert R. Boren have defined leadership as this special ability to facilitate group interaction.[15]

Trust

Effective group interaction is enhanced in an organizational climate of mutual trust. Barbara Conroy and Barbara Schindler Jones point out that people communicate better if they are working in a climate that suggests confidence, mutual understanding, and a strong sense of common purpose.[16] Studies support the conclusion that the more positive the climate, the more productive the organization.[17] It is the responsibility of a manager to establish a conducive communication climate. The ideal climate is characterized by supportiveness, participative decision making, trust, confidence, credibility, and openness and candor. All of these components are bound up in and are a product of the manager's style and system of communication.[18] A manager inspires trust and confidence through openness and integrity. Drucker has identified integrity of character as one of the most important qualities a manager can possess.[19]

Faith in the integrity of another person or trust in that person develops only when total honesty and reliability are demonstrated. Samuel A. Culbert and John J. McDonough say that the most effective management tools are trusting relationships; they are a necessary condition for the long-term effectiveness of any organization. Leaders who have the capacity to establish trusting relationships create the attitude and respect that motivates others. Good communication entails people telling one another about themselves and the needs that lie behind their wants. This sharing permits better understanding of how another sees events, what he or she hopes to achieve, and why he or she is proceeding in a specific way. A manager must strive to understand each individual's orientation and what that individual is attempting to accomplish both organizationally and personally. In today's complex organizations, it takes a great deal of effort and skill for someone to maintain a focus on another person's needs while simultaneously pursuing his or her own needs.[20]

A library manager must understand the consequences of differing motivations on the part of the staff. The trust a manager builds by exhibiting sensitivity and understanding enhances his or her ability to lead. An understanding library manager recognizes that librarians, too, march to different drummers. Not all professional librarians aspire to ever higher levels of responsibility. A sensitive library manager respects and supports the employee who is satisfied with his or her rung on the career ladder. Understanding this orientation enables the manager to communicate more effectively on any number of issues, from introducing change to evaluating performance, in a nonthreatening, productive way.

A manager must realize that although the subjective experiences of another person will never be identical to his or her own, they will be recognizably similar. Karl J. McGarry calls this faculty "the moral imagination," or "empathic communication," and sees it as the basis for the ethical maxim of do unto others as you would have them do unto you.[21]

Such an approach to communication draws on the writing of Karl Jaspers, who regards communication as the universal condition of man's being.[22] Both the Jewish theologian Martin Buber and Jaspers emphasize that the use of communication is to "commune" not to "command," and they reject the traditional approach to knowledge that the true understanding is gained by objectivity alone. On the contrary, they assert that "empathy" and "intersubjectivity" are central to effective communication.[23]

Empathy

Empathy has been defined by Kenneth B. Clark as "the capacity of an individual to feel the needs, the aspirations, the frustrations, the joy, the sorrows, the anxieties, the hurt, indeed, the hunger of others as if they were his or her own."[24] Failure to use empathy forms the basis of interpersonal and social tension and conflict. Empathy is both a physical response, such as weeping at a sad movie, and a perceptual response exemplified in the phrase, "Put yourself in your customer's shoes." This perceptual response is filtered through one's own personal experiences, so that an individual thinks and feels what he or she perceives another to be thinking and feeling.[25]

Empathy enables individuals to engage in direct joint ventures. William Howell has extensively developed the theory that empathic skills are central to competence in human interaction. He reaffirms that achieving empathy in relationships is a desirable goal for anyone who wishes to be proficient in day-to-day interaction.[26] Empathy is thus an essential attribute for a manger whose success depends on communicating effectively.

As individuals find an increasing number of things that they can share in mutually helpful ways, trust develops between them. Trust enables individuals to become less self-conscious and more spontaneous. Some risk is always involved when sharing a new kind of information in a particular relationship. Openness, which is the opposite of defensiveness, implies a commitment. Again, it is the manager's responsibility to support a climate of risk taking.

People differ in their comfort with risk taking and they will respond to the degree they perceive the organization supports them.[27] A library manager who seeks to build or maintain an open or supportive climate must behave in certain ways. He or she should strive to make statements that are descriptive rather than evaluative or judgmental and to adopt a problem-solving orientation rather than one of control. Comments that reflect empathy and honesty rather than a withdrawn neutrality are the goal. Such a manager seeks to build equality in relationships, rather than power struggles. She or he is willing to look for options rather than be limited to an either-or approach that sees only one alternative.[28]

Openness

In order to benefit from empathy in human relationships, an individual must be open and responsive to unexpected messages from others. When words are spoken in a sequence determined by earlier planning or from habit, Howell calls this part of a message "scripted."[29] Any individual who tries to anticipate what will happen and continually plans what to do next may enter an interaction with a one-track mind. He or she is closed to alternatives and is unresponsive. The script prevents him or her from noticing the unexpected. Commitment to an anticipated sequence of events limits effectiveness in adjusting to unforeseen circumstances. Howell does not suggest that effective communicators are totally "unscripted," only that they do not expect everything that was anticipated to happen.

Howell uses a model of communication that is intrinsically interaction and open ended, one that portrays continuing modification of outgoing messages by information only just received, and continually modified reception of information received caused by the most recent message sent by the receiver. When everything a communicator receives changes the next message sent, and everything sent modifies the next message unit received, interpersonal communication that is truly empathic may occur.[30]

Willingness to accept change and appreciation of innovation are not likely to become library organizational norms unless persons in leadership roles embody such behavior themselves. It is the responsibility of the leader to contribute to, often to create, a context that makes it easy for individuals in an organization to say what needs to be said. In addition to providing a role model, the leader's planning, control of environment, relations with individuals in the group, intellectual competence, and empathic abilities all combine to influence working conditions. Far more than any other, the leader determines—literally controls—these variables that limit or enhance group productivity.[31] Gerald M. Goldhaber confirms that people acquire the values of the group with which they associate.[32]

Intuition

Interactive communication requires the making of numerous decisions. Some are deliberative and some are intuitive. Howell defines intuition as the production of answers without conscious processing of data.[33] Carl Jung characterized intuition as perception by way of the unconscious.[34] Intuition makes it possible to respond quickly and appropriately to another person in an interchange. The superior interpersonal communicator finds it easy and natural to abandon planned procedures and respond with unscripted and appropriate spontaneous reactions. The rigidity of the less flexible communicator is self-imposed. An internal monitoring mechanism cautions its owner not to risk being spontaneous. In essence, a flow of conscious, obstructive, and extraneous mental activities gets in the way of fresh appropriate responses.[35] Individuals who rely on intuition perceive meanings and relationships by way of insight. They do not impose a rigid filtering mechanism, but are comfortable with a holistic approach.

A number of research instruments have been designed to provide information about individual styles of information gathering and decision making. The Myers-Briggs Type Indicator (MBTI) is one such instrument; it reflects Jung's theory of psychological types. The essence of the theory is that much seemingly random variation in behavior is actually quite orderly and consistent, being due to a basic difference in the way individuals prefer to use their perception and judgment. Perception involves all the ways of becoming aware of things, people, happenings, or ideas. Judgment involves all the ways of coming to conclusions about what has been perceived.

The MBTI contains four separate indices, each of which reflects a basic preference that, under Jung's theory, directs the use of perception and judgment. The extraversion versus introversion index affects choices as to whether to direct perception judgment mainly on the outer world or mainly on the world of ideas. Sensing versus intuition describes what kind of perception is preferred. One may rely primarily on the process of sensing, which reports observable facts or happenings through one or more of the five senses; or one may rely more on the less obvious process of intuition, which reports meanings, relationships and possibilities that have been worked out beyond the reach of the conscious mind. The thinking versus feeling index is designed to identify which kind of judgment an individual trusts when he or she needs to make a decision. The judgment versus perception index describes the process a person uses primarily in dealing with the outer world. The four indices yield sixteen possible combinations called "types."

The MBTI has been administered to thousands of individuals over the last forty years. The results have been developed into tables, which show the frequencies of types. Of particular interest in the context of this paper is the occurrence of intuitive types. Using the MBTI Data Bank, Isabel Myers determined that 75 percent of the general population in the United States prefer to rely on the senses; only 25 percent tend to rely on intuition.[36]

This research indicates that a majority of the population prefer to work analytically, to depend on known facts rather than to look for possibilities and relationships. The data gathered by Myers-Briggs research on the general population supports the idea that the ability to communicate on a intuitive level is less common. Conversely, a survey of 226 Minnesota librarians conducted in 1986 indicates that the tendency to act intuitively is much more common among librarians than among the general population. A surprising 65.5 percent of these librarians approach problems intuitively.[37]

The implication of the Minnesota study is that the personality types found in the library profession may have an advantage when it comes to developing the skills necessary for effective communication presented in this chapter. Managers who approach problem solving and information gathering intuitively, with openness and empathy, are more likely to develop a shared understanding—that is, to communicate effectively.

Leadership

Drucker has written that respect for the individual and his or her work is an essential component of leadership.[38] A leader seeks to create an atmosphere of approval and security in which subordinates feel free to express themselves without fear of censure or ridicule. He or she is sensitive to the needs and motivations of others in the organization and is able to judge the possible reactions to, and outcomes of, various possible courses of action. Having this sensitivity, he or she is able and willing to act in a way that takes these perceptions by others into account. By accepting the existence of viewpoints, perceptions, and beliefs that are different, a manager becomes skilled in understanding what others really mean by their works and behavior. He or she becomes equally skilled in communicating to others, in their own contexts, what he or she means.[39] Ultimately, a manager who practices these skills will lead the organization toward a climate of trust and openness, a climate that supports effective communication. Richard De Gennaro has written that a manager who lacks the courage to stand up for principles or stand by the hard decision will lose the trust of the staff and the right and ability to lead them.[40]

The ideal of perfect communication—that it be always clear, accurate, complete, balanced and unbiased—is unobtainable. That does not mean, however, that managers should not strive toward it or lead their organizations in its pursuit. As Sayles has written, "Only managers who can deal with uncertainty, with ambiguity, and with battles that are never won but only fought well can hope to succeed."[41]

References

1. Peter Drucker, *The Practice of Management* (New York: Harper & Row, 1954); Henry Mintzberg, *The Nature of Managerial Work* (New York: Harper & Row, 1973); Leonard R. Sayles, *Managerial Behavior: Administration in Complex Organizations* (New York: McGraw-Hill, 1964).
2. Robert L. Katz, "Skills of an Effective Administrator," *Harvard Business Review* 52 (September/October 1974): 90–102; W. Kiechel, "Harvard Business School Restudies Itself," *Fortune* 99 (June 18, 1979): 48–58.
3. Paul Watzlawick, Janet Helmick Beaven, and Don D. Jackson, *The Pragmatics of Human Communication: A Study of Interactional Patterns, Pathologies, and Paradoxes* (New York: Norton, 1967).
4. William S. Howell, *The Empathic Communicator* (Belmont, Calif.: Wadsworth Publishing Company, 1982).
5. Chester I. Barnard, *The Functions of the Executive* (Cambridge, Mass.: Harvard University Press, 1938).
6. Sayles, *Managerial Behavior*, 35.
7. Henry Mintzberg, "The Manager's Job: Folklore and Fact," *Harvard Business Review* 53 (July–Aug. 1975): 49–61.
8. David Kenneth Berlo, *The Process of Communication* (New York: Holt, 1960), 1.
9. Lowell A. Martin, *Organizational Structures of Libraries* (Metuchen, N.J.: Scarecrow Press, 1984), 61.
10. Barbara Conroy and Barbara Schindler Jones, *Improving Communication in the Library* (Phoenix: Oryx Press, 1986), 114.
11. Howell, *The Empathic Communicator*, 47.
12. Garda W. Bowman, "What Helps or Harms Promotability?" *Harvard Business Review* 42 (January–February 1964), 6–26.
13. Rudi Klauss and Bernard M. Bass, *Interpersonal Communication in Organizations* (New York: Academic Press, 1982), 2–3.
14. John P. Kotter, *Power and Influence* (New York: Free Press, 1985), 76.

15. R. Wayne Pace and Robert R. Boren, *The Human Transaction: Facets, Functions and Forms of Interpersonal Communication* (Glenview, Ill.: Scott, Foresman, 1973).
16. Conroy and Jones, *Improving Communication*, 66.
17. John P. Campbell et al., *Managerial Behavior, Performance and Effectiveness* (New York: McGraw-Hill, 1970).
18. Conroy and Jones, *Improving Communication*, 76.
19. Drucker, *The Practice of Management*, 462.
20. Samuel A. Culbert and John J. McDonough, *Radical Management: Power Politics and the Pursuit of Trust* (New York: Free Press, 1985).
21. K. J. McGarry, *Communication, Knowledge, and the Librarian* (London: Clive Bingley, 1975), 62.
22. Karl Jaspers, *Man in the Modern Age* (New York: Doubleday, 1957).
23. Martin Buber, *Between Man and Man*, trans. Ronald Gregor Smith (New York: Macmillan, 1972).
24. Kenneth B. Clark, "Empathy: A Neglected Topic in Psychological Research," *American Psychologist* 35 (February 1980): 187–90.
25. Howell, *The Empathic Communicator*, 108.
26. Ibid., 3.
27. Maggie Moore and Paul Gergen, "Risk Taking and Organizational Change," *Training and Development Journal* 39 (June 1985): 72–76.
28. Conroy and Jones, *Improving Communication*, 86.
29. Howell, *The Empathic Communicator*, 4.
30. Ibid., iii.
31. Ibid., 115.
32. Gerald M. Goldhaber, *Organizational Communication*, 4th ed. (Dubuque, Iowa: William C. Brown, 1986), 109.
33. Howell, *The Empathic Communicator*, 6–7.
34. Isabel Briggs Myers and Mary H. McCaulley, *Manual: A Guide to the Development and Use of the Myers-Briggs Type Indicator* (Palo Alto, Calif.: Consulting Psychologists Press, 1985), 12.
35. Howell, *The Empathic Communicator*, iv.
36. Myers and McCaulley, *Manual*, 45.
37. Cindy Schultz et al., "Minnesota Library Association Survey 1986: A Study of Personality Type Distribution of Minnesota Librarians Using the Myers-Briggs Type Indicator and Job Satisfaction" (photocopy; used with permission of authors), 1987.
38. Drucker, *The Practice of Management*, 160.
39. Katz, "Skills," 91.
40. Richard De Gennaro, "Theory vs. Practice in Library Management," *Library Journal* 108 (July 1983): 1318–21.
41. Sayles, *Managerial Behavior*, 259.

9

Diagnosing Communication Pathologies

Carol J. Mueller

Library leaders *tell*: "Based on my decision, here is what I want you to do."

Library leaders *sell*: "Based on my decision, here is what I want you to do because . . . "

Library leaders *consult*: "Before I make a decision, I want your input."

Library leaders *participate*: "We need to make a decision together."

Library leaders *delegate*: "You make a decision. Produce this result. Ask me before you take any action."

Communication is the process through which library leaders tell, sell, consult, participate, and delegate. It is also the process through which library leaders

share the compelling vision, a vision so attractive that all want to help make it happen;

integrate the effort so that human energy and resources of all
library staff drive in the same direction and all know the
role they play in achieving the compelling vision; and
sustain a healthy environment so that library staff are working
for the library in an atmosphere of trust, fairness, cooperation, and honesty.

Library leaders empower mediators of information at various levels of library leadership. These mediators of information assume socio-
emotional leadership as well as task leadership by forming a trust network throughout the structure of the library organization. They provide
a shared interpretation of library events. Unless library leaders give library
staff such an interpretation they will form their own interpretations that
may be inconsistent with the library leader's vision. "Great ideas" may
lose their identity by the time they are carried out unless the meaning of
the "great ideas" is communicated throughout the library.

Library leaders convey the message that library communication is a
shared responsibility of all library staff. The mediators of information also
clarify the communication responsibility of each library staff member.
Receiving the meaning of messages is a responsibility of all. Providing
input is a responsibility of all.

Library leaders recognize the need for harmony between the manifest
library, the one that is seen on the "organizational chart"; the assumed
library, the one that individuals perceive to be existing; the extant library,
the one actually existing as revealed through systematic investigation; and
the requisite library, the library as it would look if it were in accord with
the reality of the situation in which it exists.[1] To align the manifest, the
assumed, the extant, and the requisite libraries is part of the compelling
vision of library leaders.

Communications Audit

"How are we doing?" "How close are we coming to that alignment?" One
way of seeking the answer is the communications audit. The communications audit is a fact-finding, analysis, interpretation, and reporting process
that studies the communication philosophy, structure, flow, and practice
of the organization. A communications audit can uncover information
blockages and organizational hindrances. It can expose misunderstandings and help gauge present communication effectiveness. It may be broad
in scope or limited. It may be used to measure the effectiveness of com-

munication in a large organization or in a single department. It may be a personal communications audit of the library leader.

Why do a communications audit? Library leaders need to determine which individuals are being reached by various information flows, the amount and the frequency of messages sent, the rate at which the messages flow, the amount of redundancy, the efficiency of message distribution, and the extent of message distortion. Information is provided by senders at various levels of library leadership. The extent to which the information is received, interpreted correctly, passed on accurately, and acted upon properly determines the extent to which communication is taking place within the library.

The "blockage" notion, a useful concept from Gestalt psychology, suggests that an organization can be compared to a plumbing system with an interlinked pattern of pipes. Maximum effectiveness comes when the pipes are unblocked. Blockages affect the whole system and reduce overall effectiveness. The system can be improved by clearly identifying the blockages, exploring them to try to understand them, assessing the damage the blockages cause, and developing a strategy for change that will reduce or eliminate them.[2] The communications audit can be used as an evaluative diagnostic tool to begin the process of identifying blockages.

Situational responsiveness is the key to doing a useful communications audit. This requires an active-reactive, adaptive approach. One must take into account the special and unique people, circumstances, and factors in one's environment. One important situational variable is the number of staff members involved. Choosing whether the communications audit will be formative, aimed at improvement, summative, or aimed at making fundamental judgments about the status quo is a necessary activity at the outset. The design, the analysis, and the findings will all depend on the situation.

MARC Department Communications Audit

In February 1987 I structured a communications audit for the MARC Department, the copy cataloging unit in the Central Technical Services Division of the University of Wisconsin–Madison General Library System. At the time, the MARC Department had twenty-six permanent employees working on a flextime schedule that allowed them to work a forty-hour week from a choice of ninety hours, throughout the week. The flextime agreement between labor and management provided for core hours only for monthly departmental meetings.

Since I was not in the MARC Department for more than half the time department employees could choose to work, I began to wonder how well we were communicating. There were telltale symptoms in the form of open complaints. I recognized the need to look below the surface of these complaints and make a diagnosis before appling a remedy. I wanted to be sure I would not make the mistake of confusing manifestations with the real illness itself. In designing the communications audit for the MARC Department, I kept in mind that I wanted to evaluate public communication, interpersonal communication, and the affective value of communicators within the MARC Department.

My first objective was to create an awareness in the MARC Department staff that they were being communicated with in many formal and informal ways and to make them aware of the amount of such communication. In evaluating the effectiveness of communication, never underestimate the importance of telling staff when they are being communicated with, of identifying the ways in which they are being communicated with, and of getting them to agree that this is the case. During February 1987, I asked the assistant head of MARC and another staff resource person to keep a log of all interactions with MARC staff. A quick analysis of these logs made it obvious to all three of us that we were giving the most attention to staff members who demanded the most attention. We quickly devised a strategy for a more equitable distribution of our time and energies based on our joint assessment that not all demands were based on need.

The two staples of communication in the MARC Department were the document and the meeting. During February 1987, I kept track of every piece of written communication routed to the MARC Department staff. As the first part of the written communications audit, I asked the staff to evaluate these written communications. I asked staff whether they had read the specific items routed and whether they needed or wanted to see those items.

I kept track of all meetings that had been scheduled for the MARC Department staff—the monthly departmental meeting and several small group meetings. As the second part of the written communications audit, I asked the MARC Department staff to indicate whether or not they had attended the meetings that were open to them and to evaluate those meetings.

The assistant head of MARC and I attended many meetings. I reviewed all of those meetings and asked the MARC Department staff how they wanted to be informed about meetings we attended, whether they preferred receiving minutes, a summary, or only that information from each meeting that had a direct impact on their work. The assistant head of

MARC and I received minutes and summaries of meetings we did not attend but which might have contained relevant information to the MARC Department. Mediators of information throughout the library organization were called upon to reconcile varying demands for information. Some staff members wanted to know everything and some only wanted to know when the locks have been changed. I was trying to achieve a consensus, but I also wanted to be able to identify individual preferences.

In preparing the remainder of the MARC Department communications audit, I incorporated some aspects of the International Communication Association (ICA) communications audit process. The ICA communications audit process uses five measurement tools or approaches: a questionnaire survey, one-on-one interviews, communication network analysis, respondent descriptions of critical communication episodes, and a communication diary maintained by each participant. The products of the ICA audit are an organizational profile of perceptions of communication events, practices, and relationships; a map of the operational communication network, identifying potential bottlenecks and gatekeepers; verbal summaries of successful and unsuccessful communication experiences; an organizational and individual profile of actual communication behaviors, allowing comparisons between actual and perceived communication behaviors; and a set of recommendations.[3] The instruments and procedures of this audit are in the public domain. I adapted the ICA questionnaire survey and the respondent descriptions of critical communication episodes for inclusion in the MARC Department communications audit. A sample question from the audit is shown in figure 1.

Staff were further queried on the amount of information they sent and the amount of information they needed to send; the amount of information or follow-up that was, or needed to be, taken on that information; and the amount of information they received from various sources: coworkers, individuals in other parts of Central Technical Services, Acquisitions and Catalog Editing, and in departments of the General Library System outside Central Technical Services, the assistant head of MARC, the head of MARC, as well as department meetings, the weekly staff newsletter, and the "grapevine." Staff also responded to questions about the extent to which the information they received was timely; their relationships with their co-workers, the head of MARC, and the assistant head of MARC; and their level of satisfaction with their jobs.

Finally, the MARC Department staff indicated the amount of information they received from others who spoke to them personally or in small, medium, or large groups and the amount they received in writing. They were given the opportunity to express a preference for communication face-to-face one-on-one, face-to-face in a small group, face-to-face in

	This Is the Amount of Information I Receive Now					This Is the Amount of Information I Need to Receive				
	Very Little	Little	Some	Great	Very Great	Very Little	Little	Some	Great	Very Great
a. How well I am doing in my job	1	2	3	4	5	1	2	3	4	5
b. What my job duties are	1	2	3	4	5	1	2	3	4	5
c. What the priorities of my job duties are	1	2	3	4	5	1	2	3	4	5
d. How technological changes affect my job	1	2	3	4	5	1	2	3	4	5
e. How I am being evaluated	1	2	3	4	5	1	2	3	4	5
f. What my performance goals are	1	2	3	4	5	1	2	3	4	5
g. How my job-related problems are being handled	1	2	3	4	5	1	2	3	4	5
h. How GLS decisions are made that affect my job in the MARC Dept.	1	2	3	4	5	1	2	3	4	5
i. What promotion and advancement opportunities are available in GLS	1	2	3	4	5	1	2	3	4	5
j. How my job relates to the total operation of GLS	1	2	3	4	5	1	2	3	4	5

While you were filling out the previous section, the questions may have brought to mind a recent work-related experience of yours in which *communication* was particularly ineffective or effective. Please answer the questions below and give a clear summary of that experience.

a. To whom does this experience primarily relate? (circle one)
    1. Co-worker   2. Assistant Head of MARC   3. Head of MARC

b. Please rate the quality of communication described in the experience below (circle one):
    1. Effective.   2. Ineffective

c. To what item in the previous section does this experience primarily relate? _____ (put in item number)

Fig. 1. A sample questionnaire from the MARC Department communications audit

a large group, or in writing in various situations. They evaluated whether they were satisfied with the amount and kind of communication they had received and indicated specific suggestions for improvements.

Even before the results of the audit were tabulated and the analysis begun, there were positive side effects. One staff member commented after completing the audit, "That was cathartic. I feel better already." Another asked, "Why did you go through all of this effort? Things aren't that bad." Another added: "You've cooled this issue for a while." Finally, there was the placebo effect: no one complained about how they were being communicated with for several months.

An analysis of the responses revealed agreement on the amount of communication needed and the amount of communication wanted except in the area of job performance and in relationships with the rest of the General Library System. The MARC Department staff saw job performance as not merely the aggregate of skill levels as distinct tasks, but also the consistent application of effort and appropriate apportionment of work time. They considered the articulation of job duties and work standards as useful but at best considered it only a general guideline for job performance. "I have too much to do and no guide as to what not to do. I am deciding for myself what not to do. I am avoiding those parts of my job I dislike the most," commented one staff member.

The audit further revealed that departmental procedures were clearly understood. It was their application that provoked concern and desire for consultation. The MARC Department staff requested an additional resource person who would be in the department while the head of MARC and the assistant head of MARC were attending meetings.

The MARC Department staff sent a clear message that they wanted to feel like a part of the larger whole. They wanted a clearer understanding of the processing of library materials that takes place in the other departments of Central Technical Services. They wanted an information-sharing relationship with bibliographers and original catalogers.

The results of the audit provided the MARC Department with a clear vision of a number of problems. We took the approach that problems are simply situations we want to be different and proceeded through an orderly problem-solving process. We had a number of problem-solving meetings and focused on describing the problems objectively. (What's happening here?) We tried to get agreement on the problem, describing the worst, the best, and the current states of the problem. We gathered ideas without criticism, judgment, or evaluation then evaluated alternatives and combinations of alternatives. We chose solutions. We created a plan.

The plan was a reorganization of the MARC Department from one large group into four self-managing work groups. These work groups were called VIPS, Vertically Integrated Production Systems. They included all levels of the MARC Department staff and assumed responsibility for all the MARC Department activities corresponding to the existing cluster organization: Area Studies, Humanities, Sciences, and Social Science clusters—organizational units including bibliographers, member librarians, and catalogers that were a product of the compelling vision of D. Kaye Gapen, former dean of the General Library System at the University of Wisconsin–Madison. Library leaders challenge the structure of the library organization and make changes in that structure to improve library communication.

Our goals were to provide this cluster organization with an area-specific support system of copy catalogers within the existing MARC Department, to provide an additional level of support and training for the MARC Department, to provide an opportunity for the MARC Department staff to relate their work to the work of others, to assume pride and ownership of an end product, and, in so doing, to improve the MARC Department quality control and accountability.

The reorganization of the MARC Department was accomplished in several phases. The constitution of VIPS, the choice of VIPS leaders, and the preparation of VIPS leaders for their new responsibilities were included in the initial phase. The VIPS were composed of a VIPS leader and a distribution of staff classified as Library Services Assistants 2, 3, 4, and 5, and Library Associates 1 and 2. VIPS size was determined by the work load of the cluster. The MARC Department staff signed up for the VIPS of their choice. After groups were formed, several people chose to trade with someone in another VIPS after a trial period. Membership in most VIPS remained stable. VIPS members chose to serve as VIPS leaders on a two-month rotation schedule.

The next phase involved redirection of monographic and serials workflow and the creation of workflows of materials from Acquisitions Department to the appropriate VIPS in the MARC Department. The final phase was a period of observation and adjustment. Responsiveness and adaptiveness were the watchwords of this phase.

Tom Peters in *Thriving on Chaos: Handbook for a Management Revolution* offers the following as guiding premises for achieving flexibility by empowering people: "Involve everyone in everything; use self-managing teams."[4] The self-managing teams have improved communication. Staff members in each VIPS have had the opportunity to get to know one another well and to get to know one another's tasks. They have developed a unique unit cohesion and esprit de corps. Peer pressure has become a strong motivating factor. These self-managing teams have been in constant, nonabrasive contact with other cluster members throughout the

General Library System. They have exchanged visits with cluster members in member libraries of the General Library System and have attended meetings of their parent clusters. They have invited cluster bibliographers to the MARC Department to share their perspectives. MARC VIPS members have, in turn, shared their workflow and procedures with the bibliographers. They have met with cluster catalogers to discuss cataloging priorities. The MARC Department is now preparing for the second communications audit to determine if the perceptions of better communication due to reorganization are accurate.

Shared visions and values bind employees together in collaborative pursuits. Group tasks, complementary goals, and shared rewards also play a role. Tasks that require people to exchange ideas and resources reinforce the notion that participants have cooperative goals. According to James M. Kouzes and Barry Z. Posner in *The Leadership Challenge: How to Get Extraordinary Things Done in Organizations*, as individuals jointly work together, seeing they need information from one another to be successful, they become convinced that everyone should contribute and that by cooperating they can all achieve the task successfully. Employees realize their goals are cooperative when day-to-day organizational norms encourage them to share information, listen to one other's ideas, exchange resources, and respond to one another's requests through positive interdependence.[5]

Regardless of the level and the amount of staff involvement in the decision-forming process, trust in the library leader is the key to a healthy library environment. It is necessary for library leaders to build trust to accomplish extraordinary things. Library leaders communicate with words but also with actions. All library leaders need to audit their own communication from time to time:

1. Am I an optimist about the compelling vision?
2. How accountable am I?
3. How credible am I?
4. How predictable am I?
5. Am I a library leader with a good head and a good heart?
6. How do I spend my time?
7. Do I have time for people?
8. What do I reward?

Just telling today's library employees what they need to know will no longer do. Library leaders need to understand and affirm the productive, cooperative values of library staff; otherwise, unproductive, egoistic traits will undermine the library leader's vision. Psychological movements that stress self-affirmation urge today's library employees to stop feeling like a cog in a machine and to start taking responsibility for themselves. They are looking for opportunities for critical thinking, discretion, self-expression, and growth in a network of trust.

References

1. Warren G. Bennis and Burt Nanus, *Leaders: The Strategies for Taking Charge* (New York: Harper & Row, 1985), 50–51.
2. Dave Francis, *Unblocking Organizational Communication* (Aldershot, England: Gower, 1987), 13.
3. Gerald M. Goldhaber and Donald P. Rogers, *Auditing Organizational Communication Systems: The ICA Communication Audit* (Dubuque: Kendall/Hunt, 1979), 9–10.
4. Tom Peters, *Thriving on Chaos: Handbook for a Management Revolution* (New York: Knopf, 1988), 283.
5. James M. Kouzes and Barry Z. Posner, *The Leadership Challenge: How to Get Extraordinary Things Done in Organizations* (San Francisco: Jossey-Bass, 1987), 135.

10

Leadership in Libraries: Feedback as Communication

DIANNE H. WRIGHT

Communication is one of the most discussed topics in libraries. This discussion takes place in both formal meetings and in informal employee exchanges. In many libraries it is given lip service more than it is practiced. In these libraries it may sometimes seem that the only communication taking place is about the need to communicate. The various departments and activities of libraries are so interdependent that failure to communicate may have a negative impact on library service.

Although humans have communicated with each other from prehistory, the focus on communication as a science can be traced to the 1920s and 1930s. Since that time communication theories have developed and communications research has been based on the scientific method. The concept of feedback, which is an important concept in communication, was introduced by Norbert Weiner in 1948 in his book *Cybernetics*.[1]

Researchers of the early human relations movement in management supported open communication between employee and supervisor. It was believed that this communication would relieve employee stress and enable the supervisor to discover additional sources of employee motivation.[2]

This chapter will focus on the role of feedback in effective communication and will discuss ways in which feedback can assist the "supervisor" in performing his or her role as a leader. In this chapter, "supervisor" will be used to refer to all levels of management, from supervisors to directors of libraries. Leadership is expected to be a function of supervisors at every level. "Employee" will refer to all employees with the assumption that feedback should occur both from top down and bottom up. Using this terminology, the same individual could be identified as both employee and supervisor. The size of the library and the organization chart will influence how much interaction the director has with employees. It is important, however, that the director have some contact with every member of his or her staff in order to establish the leadership role and to avoid morale problems and feelings of alienation.

"Feedback is any verbal or nonverbal element that facilitates or inhibits understanding, controls or influences the flow of messages and satisfaction in interactions, and enables us to adapt or adjust those messages."[3] Any remark, any action, or even the absence of speech or action may supply feedback and may be interpreted as conveying a message. In the absence of verbal feedback, an employee will arrive at conclusions that may be incorrect. In a work relationship, feedback to the employee enables one to determine if actions are accurate and satisfactory and indicates what changes are necessary in order to perform satisfactorily. Feedback also serves as a motivator.[4]

There are many kinds of feedback: intrinsic or extrinsic, negative or positive, verbal or nonverbal, top down or bottom up. Feedback may come from a number of sources. These include the organization, the supervisor, co-workers, the task itself, and the employee. In libraries, feedback may come from patrons, trustees, deans, co-workers, or supervisors. All of these may influence the employee's attitude toward his or her job. The emphasis here is on verbal, extrinsic feedback usually from top down. The most valuable feedback is that which comes from a supervisor or someone who has an understanding of the job's requirements.[5]

Both Martin M. Greller and Philip L. Quaglieri found that feedback from supervisors ranked high among available sources of feedback.[6] Greller's study showed that employees depended most heavily on feedback from the supervisor in determining job requirements. Quaglieri's research ranked the supervisor as the second most useful source of feedback.

Performance feedback, also known in the business literature as knowledge of results, has been recognized as an important facet of employee training, performance, motivation, and satisfaction. Researchers have investigated goal setting, feedback, knowledge of results, and praise in relation to task performance.[7]

Closely related to feedback is the subject of goal setting. An examination of the library literature reveals a dearth of references to feedback or goal setting. One finds many references to information on library planning. In the planning literature there are numerous discussions about setting goals, identifying roles, and using strategic or long-range planning. Most of these references, however, discuss goals or planning for the library as an organization instead of individual goal setting. It is in the establishment and accomplishment of personal-performance goals that feedback may be most effective.

One of the most controversial, unresolved issues pertaining to feedback is this relationship between feedback and goal setting. It is not clear whether increased performance is the result of feedback or is a product of the goal-setting process. The idea that motivational effect attributed to feedback is actually due to goal setting has drawn support from a number of well-designed studies. In the majority of these studies feedback about performance in relation to the goal was always present when the effect occurred.[8]

Jay S. Kim and W. Clay Hamner conducted a study in 1976 to determine the effect of goal setting and feedback on productivity and satisfaction. The variable in the study was the amount of feedback each group received. All groups set Management-by-Objectives-type goals. The results showed that goal setting alone could improve performance without a formal feedback program. However, when self-generated knowledge of results, supervisory feedback, and praise were added to the goal-setting program, performance generally experienced a greater increase. This study gained credibility through the use of an organizational setting and the use of the same measurements of performance that the organization normally used for determining monthly efficiency. The study failed to examine feedback in the absence of a goal-setting program. This is a pertinent area of research, since part of the unresolved controversy relates to the effect of feedback alone on performance.[9]

The effect of feedback on performance has not been fully explained. A study that addressed the different aspects of feedback concluded that the exact meaning of the dimension remains highly uncertain.[10]

Tamao Matsui and Akinori Okada found that employees with low ability tended to put forth more effort when receiving goal feedback. Unless employees receive feedback, they are unable to evaluate their performance objectively. A situation without feedback would not improve performance even if goals were present.[11] Other studies have found that more difficult goals with feedback resulted in improved performance.

Improvements in performance and satisfaction that were attributed to goal setting and feedback will begin to dissipate in six to nine months.[12] Other researchers have studied the effect of feedback on persistence of task improvement. R. B. Payne and G. T. Hauty tested different feedback methods in combination with other variables, including the administration of drugs to affect performance. Under some of their test conditions, proficiency did improve for the immediate short term.[13]

It is important that library supervisors understand the relationship of change in task performance to persistency of that change. Change of short duration will require reinforcement by the continued use of feedback and reviewing goals or setting new ones. Attention to rewards and an effort to see that employees are rewarded in the manner that was promised or expected are also important in maintaining the change.

Praise is one type of feedback that the supervisor may provide, based on the employee's performance. Praise is one of the most powerful kinds of feedback available. Goals or standards for the accomplishment of a task enable the supervisor to observe the results and to offer feedback to the employee. This is extrinsic feedback, and, when positive, can be expected to strengthen the desired performance. Withholding praise for unacceptable performance should encourage the employee to improve his level of performance. This is intrinsic feedback since no overt action by the supervisor has taken place. Failure by the supervisor to give feedback on any behavior regardless of its relationship to goals or performance will eliminate the performance and motivational advantages of positive results.[14]

The library literature is rich with information about performance appraisal, also referred to as performance evaluation or personnel evaluation. Much has been written concerning the types of evaluation, when evaluations should be done, the legal aspects of evaluation, and who should be evaluated. In this context the concern is for the role of feedback in performance evaluation and how the supervisor interacts with the employee concerning the evaluation.

The most valuable aspect of performance appraisal is lost if the time and opportunity for feedback are not provided as an integral part of the process. In many libraries performance evaluation is mainly targeted for providing management data. The feedback to employees can also contribute to management's goals if it is used as a conduit that permits or encourages a two-way dialogue between supervisor and employee.

Feedback to employees should adhere to the following guidelines:

1. Express the feedback specifically and clearly.
2. Avoid a judgmental approach. Statements should be behavior-oriented.
3. Give feedback promptly. It is more effective if given close to the time at which the event occurred.
4. Focus on actions over which the employee has some control.[15]

Daniel R. Ilgen and William A. Knowlton completed research in which they tested feedback distortion to determine if evaluators inflated their ratings when they were required to give feedback to the employees being rated. It was found that supervisors do tend to give higher performance ratings when face-to-face feedback is given. Supervisors also tend to give inflated ratings when poor performance is believed to be more attributable to lack of ability than to lack of effort. The effect of these two factors would tend to result in the employee receiving a higher rating than is warranted. The ratings given seemed to be strongly influenced by the degree to which supervisors perceived that the employee did or did not work hard.[16]

Employees tend to overestimate their own performance even when clear and straightforward feedback is given. One reason for the tendency to do so may be caused by the failure to be specific in presenting feedback. Supervisors tend to consider the feedback given as more specific than does the employee. Another reason for employees seeing their performance more favorably may be caused by supervisors who gave a rating and then tried to explain it away if it was unsatisfactory. Negative feedback is unpleasant. Employees may cushion its impact by denying or downplaying the ratings. Employees who do not perform well tend to blame outside forces such as working conditions, quality of tools, and so on. Supervisors are more likely to blame the employee's lack of ability or lack of effort for poor performance.[17]

The relationship between the supervisor and the employee in the performance-feedback exchange becomes an important factor in how effective that feedback will be. The individual perceptions of each are integral to the role of feedback in the organization. Research that focused on the relationship between the status of the source of the message and the acceptance of the feedback indicated that when the feedback is positive, source status made little difference. However, status of the source is important if the message is negative.[18] High-status individuals may be able to effectively deliver negative feedback.

Two problems concerning the performance appraisal as it exists in libraries today are inadequate time and preparation for the supervisor to provide feedback and the frequency of appraisals. The frequency of performance appraisals varies, but often they are done every six months, once a year, or less frequently. The evidence indicates that the frequency and timing of the feedback affects its impact. Iglen and his associates found the variables that influenced feedback were personal characteristics such as seniority, education, age, sex, and self-esteem; employees' perceptions of the supervisor concerning power, trust, and knowledge of subordinate's job; and the feedback itself in relation to timing, specificity, consideration for employee by the supervisor, frequency, and sign (negative or positive).[19]

Feedback and performance have been studied from the viewpoint of providing feedback to employees by their supervisors. The majority of research studies have followed this configuration. The literature reports a study in which supervisors were given feedback from employees concerning their performance. Of the supervisors involved in the study, those who received feedback and set goals based on that feedback received significantly higher ratings in their performance. This illustrates that supervisors are able to respond to and profit from the same type of feedback situations that employees are. This aspect of feedback utilization warrants additional investigation.[20]

In considering the effect of feedback on self-confidence, the literature supports the fact that feedback seems to lessen women's tendencies to downgrade their prospects for success. Paulette A. McCarty undertook an investigation to verify conclusions that extrinsic feedback can raise women's self-confidence levels to equal that of men. Her results supported the theory that without feedback, women are more likely than men to lack confidence for completing a task and to judge themselves more harshly. She revealed that in situations providing feedback, women's self-confidence never reached that of men even when identical feedback was received. Women who received strong positive feedback did not reach confidence levels any higher than those held by men who received no feedback. Inasmuch as motivation is related to self-confidence, this handicaps women in achieving success in the work environment. This suggests to supervisors that precedence in providing feedback should be given to women because men may feel equally self-confident without feedback.[21]

This study has particular implications for management in libraries when one considers that the ratio of women librarians to men librarians is almost five to one.[22] If library support staff are also considered, the ratio of women to men is even greater.

Performance evaluations, when accompanied by a sound feedback program, can assist library personnel in career development and professional growth. New employees need to receive regular feedback so they may assess how well they are performing. Attention to such feedback will enable the supervisor to determine how well the employee and the job are matched. Some systems specify intervals of six months, one year, or even longer. More frequent feedback is needed to correct misunderstandings or lack of knowledge before unacceptable work habits are established.

Academic librarians who may be in line for tenure or promotion require feedback in order to know if they are developing in the areas to be evaluated. Professional growth, job performance, and overall competence may not develop as much as is necessary without information that indicates where improvements are needed.[23]

Librarians and support staff want to know about their work. One writer has noted, "Nothing seems to bother people more than just being ignored. We appear to prefer any response—even a negative one—to no response at all. Not only are people distressed when they are met with unresponsiveness; they are also discouraged from taking any initiative in the future."[24]

A consultant was hired to investigate reasons why one library was experiencing so many problems. Morale was low, many mistakes were being made, production was low, and there seemed to be little concern about service. As he talked with members of the staff, he repeatedly heard remarks such as: "Nobody knows I'm here"; "It doesn't make any difference what I do, nobody ever pays any attention"; or "Nobody tells me when changes are made." As he continued to delve into work relationships and the library operation, he soon recognized lack of communication as a major problem: The director entered and left by a side entrance and was seldom seen by anyone except his secretary and a couple of assistant directors; when he did move about the library, he was withdrawn and seldom spoke to the employees; staff meetings were seldom held, with months or even years elapsing between meetings; there were no established channels of communication; no system existed for dissemination of information.

The consultant noted these comments. He observed and listened closely to determine where information was being generated and at what point communication was breaking down. When his report was completed and recommendations were made, the director was surprised that the answer to the major problems was so "simple." Attention to exchange of information and plans for communication became a high priority. Regular meetings were scheduled, not just for the sake of meeting, but with a purpose and an agenda. It was found that there was more to talk about and share than had been expected.

The problems did not disappear overnight. Communication is never "simple," and it requires work. Gradually, with adequate feedback in both directions, conditions began to improve. Absences due to illness decreased, morale was higher, and once again the focus was on service.

Charles Bunge surveyed librarians and support staff in libraries to determine what they perceived as sources of satisfaction or sources of stress in their jobs. In an article in *Library Journal* he reported that feedback was targeted as both a source of stress and a source of satisfaction. When employees received positive feedback, including recognition and appreciation, it served as a source of satisfaction. When positive feedback was not given to the employees, its absence was identified as a source of stress.[25]

Several studies have found that the degree to which employees receive feedback concerning their success and performance is significantly and negatively correlated with burnout. Burnout was less when more feedback was given to the employees.[26]

In her book *The Librarian's Psychological Commitments*, Florence E. DeHart describes feedback as a behavioral skill and identifies three aspects of interaction relating to feedback. These are giving feedback, receiving feedback, and requesting feedback. When a person is not comfortable giving direct feedback she or he may be tempted to add an escape clause, thus compounding the problem. Giving feedback should focus on a behavior description specific enough for the other person to identify the behavior to which the first person is referring. Requesting feedback is a situation in which the employee solicits an appraisal of his or her work and service. The use of feedback in a cogent manner will reduce indirect negative feedback heard by the grapevine. Critical inquiry seeks clarification of negative criticism.[27]

Library directors generally establish the attitude toward communication within the library. The importance that they place on feedback will determine how much time and effort is devoted to providing feedback to library staff at all levels. There are many aspects to communication in libraries. Feedback is pivotal in training, goal setting, and performance evaluation. Jennifer Cargill and Gisela M. Webb have called performance evaluation an effective management tool. They identified the advantages of the process as the fostering of honest communication between supervisors and employees, the development of opportunities for feedback, the provision of a basis for appropriate continuing education, the creation of organizational support, and the fostering of improved performance that contributes to growth and development.[28]

The attention with which researchers have regarded the feedback–goal-setting–performance relationship continues to produce research studies to analyze nuances overlooked or ignored in previous studies and to examine new factors that might bear on this relationship in the organization.

The literature of management, applied psychology, and to some extent library science, provides ample evidence to persuade those responsible for leadership in libraries that feedback is one of the most effective facets of communication available to them.

Whether a library is involved in participatory management or a more autocratic approach to management, the employees find it easier to provide service and reach their goals when they are aware of what is expected of them and why. Rebecca Kroll believes that "the library which keeps everyone well informed of future plans so that staff can see where they fit into the overall scheme will have a more energetic and enthusiastic workforce than if the staff feels they 'never know what is going on.'"[29]

References

1. Werner J. Severin and James K. Tankard, *Communication Theories: Origins, Methods and Uses* (New York: Hastings House Publishers, 1979), 30–31.
2. Eric M. Eisenberg and Marsha G. Witten, "Reconsidering Openness in Organizational Communication," *Academy of Management Review* 12 (July 1987): 418–26.
3. Priscilla Diffie-Couch, "How to Give Feedback," *Supervisory Management* 8 (August 1983); reprinted in *Performance Evaluation: A Management Basic for Libraries*, ed. Jonathan A. Lindsey (Phoenix: Oryx Press, 1986), 37–41.
4. Frank J. Landy et al., "Utility Concepts in Performance Measurement," *Organizational Behavior and Human Performance* 30 (August 1982): 15–40.
5. Ayala M. Pines, "Changing Organizations: Is a Work Environment without Burnout an Impossible Goal?" in *Job Stress and Burnout*, ed. Whiton Stewart Paine (Beverly Hills: Sage Publications, 1982), 189–211.
6. Martin M. Greller and David M. Herold, "Sources of Feedback: A Preliminary Investigation," *Organizational Behavior and Human Performance* 13 (April 1975): 244–56; Philip L. Quaglieri, "Feedback on Feedback," *Supervisory Management* 25 (January 1980): 34–38.
7. Jay S. Kim and W. Clay Hamner, "Effect of Performance Feedback and Goal Setting on Productivity and Satisfaction in an Organizational Setting," *Journal of Applied Psychology* 61 (February 1976): 48–57.
8. John M. Ivancevich and J. Timothy McMahon, "The Effects of Goal Setting, External Feedback, and Self-generated Feedback on Outcome Variables," *Academy of Management Journal* 25 (June 1982): 359–72.
9. Kim and Hamner, "Performance Feedback and Goal Setting," 50.
10. Greller and Herold, "Sources of Feedback."
11. Tamao Matsui and Akinori Okada, "Mechanism of Feedback Affecting Task Performance," *Organizational Behavior and Human Performance* 31 (February 1983): 114–22.
12. Ivancevich and McMahon, "Effects of Goal Setting," 360.
13. R. B. Payne and G. T. Hauty, "Effect of Psychological Feedback upon Work Decrement," *Journal of Experimental Psychology* 50 (December 1955): 343–51.
14. Kim and Hamner, "Performance Feedback and Goal Setting."
15. John F. Kikoski and Joseph A. Litterer, "Effective Communication

in the Performance Appraisal Interview," *Public Personnel Management* 12 (December 1983) in *Performance Evaluation: A Management Basic for Libraries*, ed. Jonathan A. Lindsey (Phoenix: Oryx Press, 1986), 23–36.

16. Daniel R. Ilgen and William A. Knowlton, "Performance Attributional Effects on Feedback from Superiors," *Organizational Behavior and Human Performance* 25 (June 1980): 441–56.

17. Daniel R. Ilgen et al., "Supervisor and Subordinate Reactions to Performance Appraisal Sessions," *Organizational Behavior and Human Performance* 28 (December 1981): 311–30.

18. Keith Halperin et al., "Effects of Source Status and Message Favorability on Acceptance of Personality Feedback," *Journal of Applied Psychology* 61 (February 1976): 85–88.

19. Ilgen and Knowlton, "Performance Attributional Effects."

20. Wayne F. Nemeroff, "Utilizing Feedback and Goal Setting to Increase Performance Appraisal Interview Skills of Managers," *Academy of Management Journal* 22 (September 1979): 566–76.

21. Paulette A. McCarty, "Effects of Feedback on the Self-Confidence of Men and Women," *Academy of Management Journal* 29 (December 1986): 840–47.

22. U.S. Bureau of the Census, *1980 Census of Population, Detailed Population Characteristics, Section A* (Washington D. C.: U. S. Government Printing Office, 1984), 167.

23. Rebecca Kroll, "Beyond Evaluation: Performance Appraisal as a Planning and Motivational Tool in Libraries," *Journal of Academic Librarianship* 9 (March 1983): 27–32.

24. Pines, "Changing Organizations," 201.

25. Charles Bunge, "Stress in the Library," *Library Journal* 112 (September 15, 1987): 47–51.

26. Pines, "Changing Organizations," 201.

27. Florence E. DeHart, *The Librarian's Psychological Commitments* (Westport, Conn.: Greenwood Press, 1979), 142–45.

28. Jennifer Cargill and Gisela M. Webb, *Managing Libraries in Transition* (Phoenix: Oryx Press, 1988), 146.

29. Kroll, "Beyond Evaluation."

11

Leading through Meaning: Elements of a Communication Process

John M. Budd

It seems that leadership is most frequently defined by outward characteristics, including, and perhaps especially, by behavior with regard to communication. As Chester I. Barnard wrote in 1938:

> In an exhaustive theory of organization, communication would occupy a central place, because the structure, extensiveness, and scope of the organization are almost entirely determined by communication techniques.[1]

All management and organizational functions, indeed all human functions, depend on the process of communication. In 1949 Warren Weaver offered a simple model of communication (fig. 1).

One of the basic problems with communication is semantic, according to Weaver. That is, a problem may arise "with the interpretation of meaning by the receiver, as compared with the intended meaning of the sender."[2] There is no guarantee that what the sender of the message intends is what the receiver of that message understands.

It must be stressed that the act of communication does not involve the transmission of meaning. In any communication (technical or human), it is a *message* that is transmitted. Meaning is usually implied by the sender of the message and inferred by the receiver. There are a number of implica-

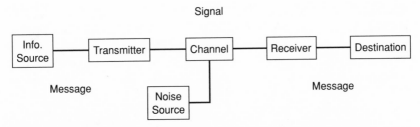

Fig. 1. Linear model of communication. Reprinted from Warren Weaver, "The Mathematics of Communication," *Scientific American* 18 (July 1949): 12–13. Used with permission

tions inherent in a discussion of meaning, as David Kenneth Berlo points out.[3] First, a message received acts as an internal stimulus and results in an internal response on the part of the receiver. Second, along with internal factors that may affect the receiver's inference of meaning, external forces may also enhance or impinge upon meaning formation. Third, in order for meaning to be inferred from a message, the receiver must share some points of reference with the sender. Fourth, meaning is not temporally fixed; the passage of time and the accumulation of experience and other stimuli may contribute to changed inferences of meaning. Finally, meaning is not spatially fixed; when a message is received by more than one person, the possibilities for uniquely inferred meaning (to a degree) increase as the number of receivers increases.

In light of these implications it seems that there are forces acting to reduce the probability of meaning inference, or inferred meaning closely resembling implied meaning. In fact, as Niklas Luhman suggests, some inevitable obstacles render meaning improbably from the outset:

> The first improbability is that, given the separateness and individuality of human consciousness, one person can understand what another means. The second improbability relates to the reaching of recipients . . . . The third improbability is the improbability of success. Even if a communication is understood, there can be no assurance of its being accepted.[4]

We can be thankful that improbability is reduced by some characteristics of communication. "Redundancy [within the process of communication] exists and entropy is reduced because [communication] constitutes a Markov process, whereby the future state is dependent upon the present."[5] If this were not true, the communication process could well result in a chaotic and anarchic situation.

With the aforementioned obstacles to meaning, it seems that the odds are against success in an organization. Anything that gets in the way of the message formulated and dispensed by the library leader to the other members of the organization can inhibit the transmission of meaning. In the discussion of inference of meaning, though, is a primary principle of phenomenology that dictates that meaning, like knowledge, is subjective. The receiver of a message employs personal, experiential, and sometimes idiosyncratic means in interpreting the message. With both internal and external obstacles at work, it is important to examine the leader's creation and transmission of the message.

A basic question remains: Can a leader emerge within an organization such as a library where the purpose of the organization is unclear, where no discernible meaning exists? It is put forth here that leadership formation is not possible where meaning is not conveyed. Every organization, every library has a top administrator, a chief executive officer, a director. Not every organization, not every library has a leader. Leadership cannot be assigned or selected on the basis of position or rank within an organization. Linda Smircich and Gareth Morgan note that "individuals in groups that evolve [common modes of interpretation and shared understanding of experience] attribute leadership to those members who structure experience in meaningful ways."[6]

The qualities of an individual that identify that person as a leader may be many and varied. One person recognized as a leader may share relatively few characteristics with another such person, even in the area of communication styles. One may be an eloquent spokesman for his or her beliefs and vision for the direction of the library; another may be able to represent graphically a sense of unified action. Whatever mode of operation or means of communication the leader chooses to employ, "the effective leader must assemble for the organization a vision of a desired future state," as Warren G. Bennis and Burt Nanus suggest.[7] This may be accomplished through rhetoric, symbology, or any other tool deemed useful and wielded successfully.

Recalling the model of the communication process mentioned earlier, we can now impart roles to some of the entities represented. The leader of the library organization, in exercising his or her ability to construct meaning and vision, assumes the part of information source. According to the model, this is the genesis of signal transmission, at which time a message, created by the leader, is sent to the destination, the members of the library organization. One of the problems with the process is that there is intervention between source and destination. The external intervention can be considerably reduced if the library leader is communicating directly with a member of the organization. With additional levels or steps placed between source and destination, the probability of success is lessened.

The external intervention may make necessary interpretation (or inference) by one or more members of the organization, then translation of that interpretation into implied meaning. At that point, the message—or some mutation of the message—is communicated to other members of the organization. The more interventions of this sort, the further is the final destination from the initial source. Also, meaning formation may be repeated several times and may not be consistent. Because of this, there is likely to be implied meaning followed by inferred meaning; then a second implied meaning based on the first inference followed by a second inference of meaning; and so on. By the time communication reaches the final destination (usually to the lower levels of the organizational hierarchy), the message received and the meaning inferred may not resemble the intention of the leader. The model in figure 2 illustrates this phenomenon:

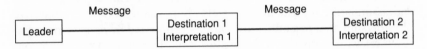

Fig. 2. Subsequent interpretation of messages

If we accept that the communication of meaning is an essential quality of a leader, the model implies that meaning, and therefore leadership, can be diffused by the interpositioning of stages between the leader's message as initially articulated and other members of an organization. What occurs in such a situation is a lack or loss of control of meaning formation (to the extent that meaning formation can be controlled at all). The leader, or would-be leader, delegates the implication of meaning to other members of the organization. For example, if the director of a library constructs a message in which he or she seeks to establish a reason for restructuring the organization of the library, but communicates that message only to the assistant and associate directors of the library, the director leaves it to these others to infer meaning from the message and to reconstruct the message for the staff of the library. What is eventually communicated may not embody the vision of the director and, furthermore, may not be consistent from one assistant director to another, as is depicted in a third model (fig. 3).

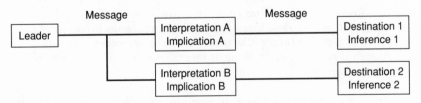

Fig. 3. Multiple interpretations of messages

These models emphasize the assertion made by Michael Maccoby in *The Leader*: "Leadership is achieved only by those who understand both their particular environment, including its social character, and their own capabilities."[8] It is essential that the library leader understand the structure of the organization and be able to alter that structure, when necessary, in order to realize the vision he or she establishes. Of course, in order to accomplish such a goal, the leader must formulate a vision for the library that is at the same time realistic, challenging, and conducive to articulation. The elements of that vision are fodder for consideration and examination elsewhere.

It is more than axiomatic that library managers are decision makers. In order to make decisions, managers have to be efficient at gathering and assimilating information. It is also important, from the perspective of leadership, that essential information be imparted by management and reach relevant segments of the organization. Does this information constitute communication of meaning? It does not, for reasons that pertain to the natures of information and meaning. As Peter Drucker states, "Where communication is perception, information is logic. As such, information is purely formal and has no meaning."[9] The difference between meaning and information is demonstrated in many segments of society, such as politics. One may argue, for example, that, as president of the United States, Jimmy Carter was more efficient at gathering and assimilating information than was Ronald Reagan. Reagan, however, upon becoming president, was able to turn ideation into ideology (more on which transformation will be said later) and to communicate the meaning of his policies to many inside and outside of government.

The difference between information and meaning is something of a dichotomy which can lead to what Orrin Klapp refers to as "meaning lag," expressed as a relationship between

> on the one hand, mere information conceived as reduction of uncertainty in any binary (yes-or-no) choice, commonly measured in bits; and, on the other, meaning as information about the relation of something to a pattern or scheme of which one is part—an awareness that is necessarily subjective. Mere information that is additive, digital, analytical, accumulates easily by being counted or categorized; whereas meaning, being subjective, and referring to synthetic or holistic properties that cannot be reduced to the sum of parts, might be called a higher sort of information that does not come easily, let alone inevitably, from a growing heap of mere information.[10]

In case a potential leader is tempted to try to foster meaning by increasing the amount of information transmitted to members of the organization, he or she should be warned that the opposite of the desired effect may occur. In fact, the overabundance of information may act as a source of noise, interfering not only with the transmission of a message, but also with the sharing of meaning. Information and meaning are not unrelated; information must be communicated for meaning to be implied and inferred. Weaver makes a suggestion, though, regarding the relationship:

> One has the vague feeling that information and meaning may prove to be something like a pair of canonically conjugate variables in quantum theory, that is, that information and meaning may be subject to some joint restriction that compels the sacrifice of one if you insist on having much of the other.[11]

The above does not denigrate the importance of information in the organization. The flow of information (including the direction of the flow) does not necessarily need to emulate the communication process designed to impart meaning. Information, being logical, formal, and frequently technical, can originate anywhere within the organization and need not be communicated to all segments of the organization. Information, however, is, more often than not, related to a function of the library, to a task performed, or to a given situation. Meaning, based on rhetoric, is hierarchically superior to information as used above; the function to which information applies depends on the meaning established by the leader.

That meaning, which is communicated to all segments of the organization (a communication that is unidirectional), is based on the vision for the library, discussed earlier. Meaning, that is, implied meaning, begins as an idea in the leader's mind. That idea may be a restructuring of the library, a redefinition of the service goals, or an incorporation of technology into the traditional mission. The idea is then developed by the leader to ensure clarity of concept and of statement. Meaning has its genesis with the clarity of thought and purpose with which the leader imbues the idea. In order to communicate meaning the leader must transform the ideation inherent in the members of the organization into an ideology to be shared. Ideology is used here to mean a systematic body of concepts common to the organizational culture.

The members of the library organization constitute a disparate group, an agglomeration of individuals with separate sets of experiences and beliefs. These individuals may also have differing notions regarding the purpose of the library. What is shared is the confluence of professional ideals, principles, and premises. These are sufficient to suggest a certain amount of agreement among individuals, but it is neither a necessary nor a sufficient condition for complete agreement regarding specific organizational objectives within a library. It is highly likely that meaning can be shared throughout an organization to the extent that disagreement and dispute are eliminated. The leader's task is to provide direction to both agreement and disagreement so that the vision is not obscured and that personal and organizational goals can be seen to act in concert.

Bennis and Nanus maintain that "leaders articulate and define what has previously remained implicit and unsaid; then they invent images, metaphors, and models that provide a focus for new attention." [12] The first part of their statement may be an overly optimistic view of the potential directedness of the organization. The organization conforming to their assessment is one that has an innate, or perhaps inert, intuition regarding purpose and direction; all that is needed is someone to give substance to the previously formless notions. A more likely scenario is one that embodies conflict and confusion to some extent. The leader in such an environment assumes a more active role, one that involves more than the awakening of a dormant, yet extant, sense of meaning. As has been stated, the leader is a communicator, an architect of meaning.

The simile of leader as architect is not original here. The concept of a leader as one able to transform the social architecture of an organization is used by Bennis and Nanus. The keystone of this architecture is meaning as is implied in their three-stage construction process:

1. Create a new and compelling vision capable of bringing the work force to a new place.
2. Develop commitment for the new vision.
3. Institutionalize the new vision. [13]

This and other ideas put forth here tacitly assume a beneficence inherent in leadership. In fact, an underlying definition of leadership at work here includes the premise that, since the leader is involved in constructing meaning that has as its end the goal of a library centered on clarity of purpose, the leader is beneficent, or he or she would not be a leader. While all of this precludes malignance, another interpretation of meaning and leadership focuses on the leader from the perspective of domination. John B. Thompson, for instance, states that

> there is evidence to suggest that very few values and beliefs are shared or accepted by all (or even most) members of a modern industrial society [and that individuals] may be enmeshed in a system of domination without recognizing that they are, or without recognizing the extent to which they are, subjected to the power of others. [14]

Thompson's interpretation hints that an absence of meaning (or the presence of confusion) is an opportunity for the ascension to a position of power by one who is able to coalesce confusion into a shared ideology. He further states that to examine this phenomenon is "to study the ways in which meaning (or signification) serves to sustain relations of domination."[15]

Perhaps the suggestions of Bennis and Nanus and of Thompson are overstated. The leader may be neither a guiding light illuminating the path of the masses with the brilliance of an idea nor a Machiavellian, achieving domination through the willingness of the masses to embrace an interpretation of meaning. For one thing, each of the views hints at an ease with which implied meaning becomes inferred meaning and is accepted by members of the organization. Each also implies a static nature for meaning; once communicated and accepted, the direction of the organization is set. Earlier reference was made to the communication *process*. Process is not static; it is dynamic and fluid. It was also stated earlier that meaning is not fixed. Yet another complication is the fact that an organization such as a library is dynamic as well. Its processes are neither temporally nor spatially fixed. One way in which this potential difficulty manifests itself is the incorporation of new members into the library organization. The socialization process by which these individuals attain full membership may or may not include inference of meaning. Success, from the library perspective, is more likely when the communication process does not exclude these individuals.

How, then, can meaning be an effective tool in an organization? The literature of organization theory includes some possibilities. One way may be through the genesis and development of coincident meaning. Barbara Gray, Michel G. Bougon, and Anne Donnellon elaborate on this notion:

> Meanings come to coincide when, through the course of regular social interaction, members begin to favor one subjective interpretation over others. In this way members generate coincident expectations about patterns of reciprocal behavior. Repeated confirmation (by oneself and by others) that those reciprocal behaviors produce the anticipated outcomes leads members to assign meaning to the behavior . . . .
> When expectations and actual behaviors among members repeatedly coincide, and if they are consistent with members' explicit and tacit self-interests, then the interpretive schemes underlying them become crystallized.[16]

Coincident meaning can constitute a rather fragile state for the library. The forces that acted to cause meanings to coincide could act to cause them to diverge. In an environment governed by coincident meaning there are competing or contradictory meanings that can lead to the deconstruction of meaning for the organization. It is the leader's task to control these contradictory meanings, to communicate an implied meaning that can be incorporated into the actions of the library staff.

An alternative to shared meaning may exist and may be effective at generating outcomes desired by the leader. This alternative is what Donnellon, Gray, and Bougon term "equifinal meaning":

> Equifinal meanings . . . are interpretations that are dissimilar but that have similar behavioral implications. When organized action follows the expression of such dissimilar interpretations, we refer to these interpretations as equifinal meanings. That is, organization members may have different reasons for undertaking the action and different interpretations of the action's potential outcomes, but they nonetheless act in an organized manner.[17]

This situation is even more fragile than that governed by coincident meaning. It is yet one more removed from true shared meaning (that is, conceptualization of the vision of the leader and action based accordingly). Equifinal meaning may be seen as functionally apposite to shared meaning, but it is quite different cognitively and motivationally. In fact, equifinal meaning may be largely accidental. As such, the behavior of the members of the organization could diverge if action is altered, even though original interpretation may be consistent. In the short term, equifinal meaning may be effective, but there is less motivation (conscious or unconscious) for organized action.

Some of the purposes of this chapter have been to point out some basic characteristics of the communication process, some of these difficulties or obstacles inherent in organizational communication, and the importance of meaning as a component of the communication process and to organizational effectiveness. One of the functions of meaning formation is the minimization of what Michael D. Cohen and James G. March call "organized anarchy."[18] Meaning formation succeeds to the extent that it can marshal unity of concept and clarity of purpose into organized action. The leader's role in this process is primary; the initial cognitive structure of meaning belongs to the leader, and it is up to him or her to communicate that meaning to the members of the organization. The difficulties of the process and functional alternatives have also been illustrated. In isolated instances or short-term action the alternatives may present a facade of success, but it is important to keep in mind Klapp's admonition, which serves as an effective closing caveat, "In a crisis of meaning, people find much that doesn't make sense, little that is basic or reliable to hold onto [sic]."[19] Success in a library depends, not merely on the avoidance of crisis, but on the initiative of meaning, which is both a function and a definition of leadership.

References

1. Chester I. Barnard, *The Functions of the Executive* (Cambridge, Mass.: Harvard University Press, 1938), 91.
2. Warren Weaver, "The Mathematics of Communication," *Scientific American* 181 (July 1949): 11.
3. David Kenneth Berlo, *The Process of Communication* (New York: Holt, 1960), 184.
4. Niklas Luhman, "The Improbability of Communication," *International Social Science Journal* 33 (1981): 123–24.
5. John M. Budd, "The User and the Library: A Discussion of Communication," *The Reference Librarian*, forthcoming.
6. Linda Smircich and Gareth Morgan, "Leadership: The Management of Meaning," *Journal of Applied Behavioral Science* 18 (1982): 258.
7. Warren G. Bennis and Burt Nanus, *Leaders: The Strategies for Taking Charge* (New York: Harper & Row, 1985), 141.
8. Michael Maccoby, *The Leader* (New York: Simon & Schuster, 1981), 59–60.
9. Peter Drucker, *Management: Tasks, Responsibilities, Practices* (New York: Harper Colophon Books, 1985), 487.
10. Orrin Klapp, "Meaning Lag in the Information Society," *Journal of Communication* 32 (Spring 1982): 58.
11. Weaver, "Mathematics of Communication," 15.
12. Bennis and Nanus, *Leaders*, 39.
13. Ibid., 141.
14. John B. Thompson, *Studies in the Theory of Ideology* (Berkeley: University of California Press, 1984), 192–93.
15. Ibid., 194.
16. Barbara Gray, Michel G. Bougon, and Anne Donnellon, "Organizations as Constructions and Destructions of Meaning," *Journal of Management* 11 (1985): 88–89.
17. Anne Donnellon, Barbara Gray, and Michel G. Bougon, "Communication, Meaning, and Organized Action," *Administrative Science Quarterly* 31 (March 1986): 44.
18. Michael D. Cohen and James G. March, *Leadership and Ambiquity*, 2d ed. (Boston: Harvard Business School Press, 1986), 2–4.
19. Klapp, "Meaning Lag," 56.

12

Mediation: A Language of Leaders

ROSEMARY HUFF ARNESON

Conflict is one of our most difficult areas for communication because we generally feel strongly about the issues involved in the situation. Faced with a conflict between two people, a leader must be able to facilitate continuing communication between those two people if a resolution is to be reached. One method for helping individuals resolve conflict is the mediation process.

The four-step mediation process has been used successfully to resolve conflicts between individuals involved in legal disputes, including separation and child-custody agreements. Mediation skills have been taught to school children and college students so that they can help their peers reach agreements. Community mediation centers are extending their training efforts beyond the professional community to include all of the area's residents.

This chapter will outline the potential uses of mediation as a management and communication tool by examining the four steps of the mediation process: introduction, storytelling, problem solving, and agreement. It will discuss ways library managers can use mediation techniques to resolve disputes between staff members, between a staff member and a patron, and between the library and other parts of the parent organization. Finally, the opportunities available for mediation training for library managers and for library staff will be examined.

The Nature of Conflict

Conflict occurs when there are differences between people, groups, organizations, or nations that, if they persist, keep the parties from coming together. In an organization such as a library, conflict can keep staff dissension high and morale low if it is allowed to continue with no effort toward resolution. Stress increases and performance diminishes, and the library manager finds himself/herself spending a disproportionate amount of time on the issue causing the conflict.[1]

Our experiences with and social views of conflict concentrate on the negative aspects of conflict. We see conflict as a win-lose situation in which one party can only achieve his or her goals at the expense of the other disputant. However, used well, conflict can be creative and positive.[2] By allowing both parties to express their points of view without the assumption that one party is right and the other wrong, the relationship between the two people can be strengthened. Jay Folberg and Alison Taylor refer to the process of resolving conflict as *convergence*: "The aims, processes, methods, or behavior that create order, stability, and unity of direction."[3]

In a library, conflict can exist between staff members, between two or more units of the organization, between a staff member and a patron, or between the library and its parent organization. Unresolved, these conflicts can adversely affect staff morale, decision making on important issues, public relations, and administrative support. Creative use of the conflict, however, can bring about a greater sense of unity and commitment to the library's goals.

Mediation Defined

Conflict management and conflict resolution are often used interchangeably in the literature, but there are important differences between the two. Folberg and Taylor state:

> *Conflict resolution* creates a state of uniformity or convergence of purpose or means; *conflict management* only realigns the divergence enough to render the opposing forces less diametrically opposite or damaging to each other.[4]

Mediation is one form of conflict resolution and has been defined as "the process by which disputants attempt to reach a consensual settlement of the issues in dispute with the assistance and facilitation of a neutral resource person or persons."[5] A key feature of the mediation process is that the disputing parties are responsible for the agreement that is reached. The mediator guides the process and provides the structure within which agreement can be reached, but he or she does not make the agreement happen. Because the agreement is personal and consensual, the disputants are more likely to accept it. Participation in the mediation process helps to reduce the tension between the people in conflict by encouraging more open and direct communication. The process also provides a model the disputants can follow when conflicts arise in the future.[6] Charles J. Tripp articulates four widely accepted principles of mediation:

> First, disputing parties cannot be forced to participate in or comply with agreements derived through the use of mediation. They must participate and comply voluntarily. Second, agreements that disputants create for themselves are not binding. Third, mediators can facilitate the activities through which disputing parties resolve conflicts and arrive at mutually satisfactory conclusions, but they have no authority to decide what disputants should do to resolve their difficulties, and they have no enforcement powers. Fourth, the mediator's role is centered on presiding over and assisting the process through which disputing parties arrive at their own decisions and resolutions through collaborative problem solving.[7]

Mediation differs from other forms of conflict resolution or conflict management in many respects. Unlike therapy or counseling, it involves conflicts between two or more people, not the personal conflicts or patterns of behavior each person experiences.[8] The adversarial processes of adjudication and arbitration are generally public and formal, with a strict set of rules to be followed. A third party is involved in the process, but he or she plays the role of decision maker, deciding which party wins and which one loses.[9] Negotiation often involves the use of designated representatives, such as lawyers. In negotiation, each side of the dispute formulates a position and winning that position means the defeat of the other person's position.[10]

Uses for Mediation

The use of third parties to resolve conflict is not new. Chinese, Japanese, and African cultures share a tradition of informal conciliation. The Jewish and Christian communities often called upon the rabbi or priest to serve as a mediator in disputes between members of the congregation.[11]

As our society has become more and more litigious, the legal community has come to recognize the need for alternatives to the formal legal process. Mediation is used in many communities as one such alternative; neighborhood arguments and landlord-tenant disputes that otherwise would consume costly time in small-claims courts are being resolved at neighborhood mediation centers. Several states now require parents working out child-custody agreements to use mediation before going to court.

Recently, mediation has begun to move into new arenas. In Rockingham County, Virginia, children in the elementary schools are learning mediation skills, which they, in turn, teach to their peers. James Madison University in Harrisonburg, Virginia, created a campus mediation center in 1987 to help students learn the techniques of mediation and to give them an alternative means for settling disputes.

The Mediation Process

The mediator's role is to guide the disputants while allowing them the opportunity to find their own solutions to the problems. Generally, a mediation session is attended by the disputants and one or more mediators. When there are two disputants involved, many mediators find that using two mediators helps in building rapport. Mediation takes place in a neutral setting: a mediation center, the mediator's office, a library conference room. The site should have comfortable seating with space available for breaks and private consultations between the mediator and one of the parties. Some disputes are settled in a single session; others, particularly those involving complex issues, may require a series of sessions before agreement is reached.

During the *introduction* phase, the mediator sets the stage for the mediation session. He or she reviews what will happen during the session and explains that the goal of mediation is for the disputing parties to reach an agreement with which they are both comfortable. It is also during this stage that the mediator explains the ground rules to be followed. While the use of most ground rules, such as no smoking or no name-calling, vary from mediator to mediator, the rule of allowing each party to speak without interruptions is common to all. The mediator uses the introduction phase to explain his or her role and lets the parties know that any agreement reached through mediation is theirs, with the mediator acting as the facilitator for that agreement.[12] Other issues covered during introduction include confidentiality, fees and payment for the mediator's services when applicable, the potential need for individual consultations with the disputants, the mediator's need to take notes during the session, and the procedures for reviewing the agreement.[13]

Once the mediator is sure that both parties understand the mediation process and the ground rules for the session, he or she moves on to the next phase: storytelling. During this stage, each disputant has the opportunity to tell his or her side of the story. The mediator needs to elicit not just the facts as each person perceives them, but also their feelings about the situation bringing them to mediation and about any underlying causes for the immediate conflict. The most important skill for a mediator to use during storytelling is listening. The mediator should be sensitive to the nonverbal messages expressed through body language, tone of voice, and facial expression. [14]

During storytelling, it is important that the disputants address all the issues, and it is up to the mediator to make sure this is done. [15] A dispute between two staff members may seem to be about the use of their joint closet only, but may in reality involve work assignments and feelings of resentment about merit increases. Unless all the issues are addressed, the agreement reached will stand little chance of success. The use of open-ended questions and questions regarding the disputants' feelings about an issue can help bring out these underlying concerns. It should also be noted that most conflicts have some sort of history; the issue that brings the disputants to mediation is probably not the first one that has created conflict between two people involved. If the mediator is a colleague of the disputants, he or she may already be aware of some of these issues. Through careful questioning, the mediator brings out these past issues in addition to exploring the current cause of dispute.

Once all of the issues have been explored and both parties have had a chance to say all they need to say, the mediation session can turn toward solutions. Ronald S. Kraybill suggests that the mediator conclude story-telling by asking both parties what they want to see happen as a result of mediation. [16] This delineation of goals leads naturally into the *problem-solving* stage of the mediation process. At this point, the mediator may summarize the positions of each disputant and then ask them both if they are ready to move toward finding a solution. Next the parties, with the assistance of the mediator, list the issues involved in the conflict. The mediator may want to highlight those issues on which both parties already agree. For example, he or she may say, "It seems that you both want to give the best service to the library's patron as is possible," or, "You agree that patron service is a top priority in the circulation department." Sometimes the only obvious point of agreement may be that both people want to end the dispute, but highlighting it establishes that there is some degree of common ground between the two positions.

Once all the issues have been listed, with suggestions coming from the disputants as well as the mediator, the mediator can suggest that they address the first issue. Issues should be addressed one at a time; any issues not noted before, but which arise in the discussion of another issue, should be added to the list. As the issues are discussed, both parties will begin to suggest solutions, and the mediator should encourage this. The mediator should not be reluctant to suggest solutions as well, since his or her perspective on the dispute is fresh and impersonal.[17] As the discussion continues, one or both parties may begin to offer "If . . . then" suggestions, such as "*If* she will ask my permission before borrowing things from my desk, *then* I would be willing to work on the project with her." The mediator needs to listen for these suggestions and use them in formulating the agreement. When a suggestion such as the one illustrated above is made, the mediator can say, "John, you're saying you'd be willing to work with Mary on the project if she will ask your permission before she borrows things from your desk. Mary, would you be willing to agree to that?" If Mary and John both agree to these statements, then the mediation session can move forward into the *agreement* stage.

Agreement is not always easy to reach. When an impasse is reached, the mediator may wish to talk with both parties privately. When alone with the mediator, a disputant may be more willing to show flexibility than when he or she is in front of the other party. The mediator may also need to remind one or both disputants of the cost of not reaching agreement.[18] In a work situation, this may be as inconsequential as having to take an earlier coffee break or as serious as losing a job.

The final stage of mediation in *agreement* is the preparation of a formal, written statement of what each party will do or not do, with stated deadlines. This agreement should be the creation of both disputants, not of the mediator, even though the mediator has invested a great deal of his or her time and energy into the mediation process. As Kraybill states, "The greater [the disputants'] sense of ownership of what has been hammered out, the greater the likelihood of long-term reconciliation."[19]

The mediation process does not end when an agreement has been signed. "The mediated plan must often be submitted to superiors, committees, boards of directors, executives, or other authorities for final ratification."[20] The mediator will also want to check back with both parties at regular intervals (these can be stated as part of the agreement) to see how well the agreement is working. While both parties may have signed the agreement with the best of intentions for seeing it through, unforeseen circumstances can arise that put the agreement in jeopardy. With the help of the mediator, the disputants can use the mediation process they experienced to deal with these new areas of conflict.[21] Mediation does not always work, and the parties may not be able to continue in anything but the most formal of relationships, if they are able to maintain a relationship at all. However, the success rate for mediation has been quite high, and people who have been through the process have reacted well to it. Studies and postmediation evaluations show a high degree of agreement, satisfaction, and willingness to use mediation again.[22]

Library Applications for Mediation

Libraries, like all other organizations, experience conflicts. These conflicts occur at a variety of levels. The mediation process can serve the library manager as one of several tools used to address conflicts at all these levels.

Disputes between staff members are among the most common kinds of conflict a manager has to face. When people spend the majority of their waking time together, conflict is inevitable. However, these conflicts can interfere with the operations of the library department and with the performance level of both employees. As other employees become involved in the conflict, either as participants or witnesses, morale is also effected. In this case, the supervisor can use the implied power of his or her position to step in and mediate the conflict. The disputing parties know that if they do not reach a solution, the supervisor may impose one upon them.[23] By using the mediation process, the supervisor can lead the disputants to a solution that addresses both their needs and the goals of the department. Two staff members may have to share an office, and only one of them is a smoker. If the other person objects to cigarette smoke, the two are in conflict. Instead of arbitrarily stating that smoking will or will not be allowed in the office, the manager to whom these two people report may choose to use mediation to resolve the conflict. Mediation will allow both people the opportunity to express all their feelings about the situation; perhaps the smoker feels the office mate spends too much time on the telephone. Mediation allows the supervisor and both disputants to explore all the options, from setting times of day when each person will use the office to switching their offices with other staff members for whom smoking or telephone use will not be an issue. Reaching the agreement in a case such as this one can be a creative process, and one in which all the concerned parties participate. By becoming a part of the solution, the two parties move from hostile disputants to cooperative participants, and they may find themselves becoming excited about both the mediation process and the solution they reach.

Disputes between supervisors and employees arise almost as frequently as those between peers on the library staff. Because of the power inherent in the supervisory position, the parties begin the conflict in unequal positions. The mediation process, because it addresses the needs and concerns of both people involved in the dispute, can serve as an equalizer in these situations. The supervisor must bring a willing and cooperative attitude to mediation; he or she must be willing to give up a degree of power in the interest of conflict resolution. The staff member who sees that he or she will be treated as an equal to the supervisor will be more willing to discuss the issues involved in the conflict and more willing to reach an agreement. If the staff member perceives that the supervisor is going to take the attitude of "I'm the boss, therefore I'm right," he or she may block the agreement in an effort to counteract that expression of power. In a conflict between employee and supervisor, the use of co-mediators would be warranted, especially if one mediator is in a supervisory position and the other is not. Both parties then feel they have a sympathetic ear to hear their stories.

Many members of a library's staff spend their days in contact with the public, not all of whom are friendly and pleasant in their dealings with the library staff. Arguments about fines, lost books, and other library policies arise. In the interest of both staff morale and good relations with the public, the library manager may need to intervene in some of these conflicts. For example, the head of the reference department may hear a reference librarian and a patron arguing about the library's policy of not allowing reference books to be taken from the library. Clearly, there is a conflict here. The reference librarian needs to enforce the library's policies consistently; the patron needs access to the information in the reference source. By intervening in this dispute and playing the role of the mediator, the head of the reference department can listen to both parties, hear about any underlying sources of conflict (the patron has a record of not returning books, for example) and help the librarian and the patron reach an agreement. Because he or she is mediating from a superior position—head of the reference department—the mediator in this case has more latitude to suggest or endorse agreements that may fall outside a strict interpretation of library policy.

Most libraries are parts of a larger organization: a city or county government, a college or university, or a large corporation. Because the resources of that larger organization are finite, the library must compete with the other units of the organization for a reasonable share of those resources. Many times discussions on budgets and allocations become negotiating sessions; each unit states its needs, and those needs are treated as mutually exclusive. If the library gets what it needs, then the English department does not. The skills used in mediation can help turn these discussions from negotiating sessions focused on each unit's position to a discussion of the overall goals and objectives of the organization. For example, the English department may have requested money for a word processing lab to support the university's computer literacy goals; the library has requested money for additional staff for its microcomputer lab. Through mediation, the two units may find a creative resolution to their conflicting needs: If the library gets additional staff and some funding to purchase word processing software, it will extend the hours of its microcomputer lab to give more students access to machines needed to complete their papers. The library "wins" because it gets the staff it needs to operate the micro-computer lab; the English department "wins" by getting a word processing facility that the department does not have to staff and maintain.

Mediation can help a library manager resolve the conflicts that arise within the library; it can also be a useful service to offer to the library's patrons. The Carnegie Library of Pittsburgh has established Library Mediation Centers in three inner city branches that community residents use to resolve "backfence" and consumer disputes. The centers provide training as well as sites for mediation sessions. Patrons who have used the services of one of the centers have found that the library provides a congenial atmosphere for mediation; it is a formal but neutral setting that is also a part of the community in which the disputants live.[24]

Mediation Training

In order to learn the techniques and skills used in mediation, formal training is necessary. Established mediation centers in many communities offer training programs to introduce people to the mediation process and to give them practice through role playing in using mediation skills. Some offer specialized training tailored to the needs of an organization. In addition, organizations such as the National Academy of Conciliators, the Conflict Resolution Center, the National Center for Mediation Education, and the American Arbitration Association offer either formal training programs or can refer interested people to such programs. More and more academic courses are being offered in mediation, many as part of the graduate curriculum in law, social work, or counseling. Any training program in mediation should offer the following:

1. An examination and understanding of conflict and how individuals deal with conflict.
2. Stage-by-stage review of mediation procedures.
3. Review of the skills involved in mediation, including listening and rapport building.
4. Substantive knowledge relating to legal issues and procedures.
5. Overview of mediation ethics and standards of practice.[25]

Conclusion

Mediation cannot be the only tool available to a library manager dealing with conflict; not every situation will lend itself to mediation, and mediation does not always lead to agreement. However, mediation can be an effective tool in many conflict situations for the following reasons:

1. Mediation treats both parties as equals. Neither person is assumed to be right or wrong, and both have the opportunity to express their feelings and to have their needs met.
2. The agreement reached is worked out by the disputants themselves, not imposed by a higher authority.
3. The process encourages the disputants to examine the underlying causes of their conflict and to deal with all the issues involved, not just the cause of the immediate conflict.
4. Mediation is flexible, and the techniques of mediation can be adapted to a variety of situations.
5. Mediation is creative; it encourages the disputants to explore all the possible solutions to a problem before an agreement is reached.
6. Mediation is new to many of us; it can be an exciting alternative to traditional problem-solving techniques.

Today's libraries are dynamic and changing organizations serving an increasingly diversified and sophisticated clientele. They are exciting places to work, but the very sources of that excitement—particularly the rapid change in our services and technologies—can create conflicts. Strong leadership is needed to help libraries cope with their changing environments and to help the people within the library deal with the conflicts arising from the changes they experience. Mediation provides library's leaders with a nontraditional and exciting process for resolving conflicts as they arise.

References

1. Fred Edmund Jandt, *Win-Win Negotiating: Turning Conflict into Agreement* (New York: Wiley, 1985), 101.
2. Jay Folberg and Alison Taylor, *Mediation: A Comprehensive Guide to Resolving Conflicts without Litigation* (San Francisco: Jossey-Bass, 1984), 19.
3. Ibid., 24.
4. Ibid., 25.

5. Jay Folberg, "Mediation Overview: History and Dimensions of Practice," *Mediation Quarterly* 1 (September 1983): 8.
6. Folberg and Taylor, *Mediation,* 9.
7. Charles J. Tripp, "Intraorganizational Conflict Mediation: The Effects of Communication, Complaints, Compliance, and Confidence," *Mediation Quarterly* 7 (March 1985): 87–88.
8. Folberg, "Mediation Overview," 3.
9. Janet Rifkin, "Teaching Mediation: A Feminist Perspective on the Study of Law," in *Gendered Subjects: The Dynamics of Feminist Teaching,* eds. Margo Culley and Catherine Portuges (Boston: Routledge & Kegan Paul, 1985), 101–2.
10. Folberg and Taylor, *Mediation,* 30.
11. Folberg, "Mediation Overview," 4–5.
12. Ronald S. Kraybill, *Repairing the Breach: Ministering in Community Conflict* (Scottsdale, Pa.: Herald Press, 1980), 62.
13. Folberg and Taylor, *Mediation,* 43.
14. Kraybill, *Repairing the Breach,* 64.
15. Folberg and Taylor, *Mediation,* 48.
16. Kraybill, *Repairing the Breach,* 64.
17. Folberg and Taylor, *Mediation,* 52.
18. Kraybill, *Repairing the Breach,* 68.
19. Ibid., 70.
20. Folberg and Taylor, *Mediation,* 63.
21. Ibid., 66.
22. Ibid., 11–13.
23. Ibid., 134–35.
24. Margaret C. Albert, "A Library Where the Fighting Stops: Can Libraries Serve Their Communities as Mediation Centers?" *American Libraries* 18 (November 1987): 822.
25. Folberg and Taylor, *Mediation,* 236–42.

Part 3 ○◆○
◆◆
○◆○

Futuristic Considerations

If you don't know where you are going, you will end up somewhere else.

Laurence Peter

The chapters in this section focus on communication and leadership in libraries in the 1990s and beyond. While management deals with day-to-day matters, leadership is responsible for charting the future direction of the library. And as has been articulated in the preceding chapters, it is most difficult to expect effective leadership without effective communication. If one had to name a single, all-purpose instrument of leadership it would be communication. Leaders communicate to move people to action, to calm them in moments of panic, to explain setbacks and so on. Although the most inspired leadership communication is probably possible only among leaders with exceptional gifts, most of the communication necessary for leadership can be taught. Where leadership development is the goal, the most effective arena for personal growth continues to be the workplace. As Norman Douglas put it, "There are some things you can't learn from others. You have to pass through the fire." It is not really a mystery why several librarians fade before fulfilling their leadership potential. The fulfillment of promise in "real life" is dependent upon attributes other than talent: courage, resolve, emotional stability, steadiness, and capacity to stay the course. Finding role models for young librarians who want to be leaders in their chosen profession is one important way to enhance library leadership. There is much about communication and leadership that can be learned from living examples. Mentors are leaders who are willing to help a young person over a period of time in a one-on-one relationship—as a friend, advisor, teacher, coach, listener, or resource person. Mentorships may be as formal as a master-apprentice relationship or as informal as an older and younger friend.

Library leaders in the 1990s will have the responsibility of changing the culture of libraries. For example, technology will provide an opportunity for librarians to create more user self-sufficiency mechanisms. Greater emphasis must and will be placed on being more creative and increasing productivity. These noble goals will require an even more sophisticated communication process. The articulation of aspirations, formulation of strategies to realize goals, and the creation of the library's future all demand fluid communication between the leaders and followers.

Internally, if a library is to remain vital it must have easy, open communication among all of its divisions/departments. Often libraries create rigid internal walls that block free communication. The leader's task is to restore open communication.

Just as the library tends to diminish effective internal communication, so it tends to cut communication with the outside world. It does less listening, but that is not the main problem. The main problem is that the increasingly dogmatic convictions it entertains serve to filter information from the outside world. This is unfortunate because messages from outside (e.g., from publishers and vendors) can be a significant mode of testing reality as well as a stimulus to renewal. From outside comes word of competitive pressures, adverse reactions, alternative solutions. The leader's task is to open the doors and windows.[1]

Designing the future for the library and creating ways to make that future happen is a formidable task for any leader. On the one hand, too many leaders are only great dreamers. They have a vision, but they cannot or choose not to articulate that vision in a meaningful way to their constituents or followers. On the other hand, those leaders who have the ability and desire to share their vision with others do so in written or verbal communication. These same leaders put heavy emphasis on the intangibles of vision, values, and motivation and understand intuitively the nonrational and unconscious elements in the leader-constituent interaction. Truly great leaders continue to grow and change over the course of their active careers.

Change and innovation normally result in an end to the status quo. With the new technology, which is causing many positive changes in libraries, there has emerged a prevailing apprehension that it will dehumanize the library. Some believe that the machine will replace the librarian. The leader must be conscious of the impact these modifications will have on the human dimension. Attitudes, skills, and habits of mind are all at stake during change. The effective leader will employ the various components of communication while initiating and implementing change. Examples may include meeting with the entire library to articulate new goals and objectives, distributing an appropriate written communiqué on a new project, incorporating innovative endeavors in the library's long-range plan, meeting with individual staff members, or a combination of these activities. The trick is to meld communication with leadership. There should not be any surprises associated with change.

The attainment of excellence in services will surely be a goal in the repertoire of library leaders during the 1990s. Just what this concept of "attainment of excellence . . . " means will be left to the leader for articulation. Breaking through the "good enough" barrier to enter the zone of "excellence" requires total preoccupation with quality from everyone in the library. It starts with the leader's attitude. The leader's insistence on and articulation of "excellence" will be crucial. Communication of expectations is the key in realizing the library's aspirations.

The following story illustrates that leadership is certainly about being in front rather than behind one's followers:

"Pardon me, old-timer, but I was just wondering if you've been sitting there on the front porch very long."

"Yep! I reckon I been sitting here about ten years now. I sit here every day . . . just sort of watching folks pass by."

"That's good because I want to ask you if you've seen a group of marchers go by here."

" 'Bout twenty-five of them."

"Yes! Twenty-six exactly!"

"All dressed alike? Wearing funny little hats like yours?"

"Yes! That's the group. Have you seen them?"

"They passed through here yesterday about this time. They were heading east and making pretty good time."

"Thanks, old-timer. I guess I'd better get a move on if I'm going to catch up with them."

"Hold on a minute, young fellow. Why do you want to find those folks, anyhow?"

"Why, I've got to catch up with them soon, old-timer. I'm their leader!"

Reference

1. John W. Gardner, *Renewing: The Leader's Creative Task* (Washington, D.C.: Independent Sector, 1988), 13.

13

Changing Organizational Cultures in Libraries through Effective Leadership Communication

GISELA M. WEBB

Libraries as organizational entities are in a state of transition. The prevalent hierarchical structures through which they have traditionally achieved organizational goals are no longer adequate to respond to rapidly changing environments and to solve the increasingly complex problems caused by technological advancements, the information proliferation, shrinking resources, and highly educated employees who expect more control over their work.

Libraries are entering this transition after a period of organizational stability created by long tenures of many directors, who, toward the end of their careers, concerned themselves primarily with preserving the organizational status quo. As an increasing number of these long-term library directors retire, their parent institutions and staffs are looking for new "leadership with vision and the ability to get the vision implemented."[1] The leadership qualities of their potential successors are appraised based on their records as change agents, their management styles, and their ability to handle complex human-resources problems. The proliferation of discussions and descriptions of organizational innovations at professional library conferences and in the literature attests to an increased change of momentum, which in turn creates new expectations and stress in those anticipating or already involved in the change process.

Hopes and tensions abound in today's libraries. Risk takers are energized by the prospect of change and are eager to move forward and experiment. Others who have chosen the profession to meet strong security needs are frustrated by the lack of clear directions and an uncertain future. All, however, are looking for strong leadership to harness their dormant energies, alleviate their anxieties, "infuse the organization with purpose and direction, motivate members of the organization toward realization of organizational goals, and to influence positively the perceptions which the environment holds regarding the organization."[2] All expect to play an active role in this process of recreating their organizations.

During this period of transition the challenges for library leaders are exciting and manifold. They are required to embody the values, hopes, and ambitions of library staffs and need the ability to translate them into a new organizational vision. They will be asked to dismantle outdated organizational strutures, to institute enlightened managerial practices, and to guide their staffs in creating new services and systems. To meet these challenges, the new library leaders will have to be excellent communicators. They will need to use verbal, nonverbal, symbolic, and written communication to embrace the forthcoming struggle with conflicting values and goals. They will have to listen carefully to discern emerging organizational and human-resources issues, act as role models and mentors, provide opportunities for professional and personal growth, use and share their power to build a new social fabric and order, and inspire their staffs to contribute toward a cause greater than themselves.

Creating a New Organizational Culture: Values and Maturity

The development of a new organizational culture must be based on a real need for change in a library. Most likely, new leaders will have been chosen because they are perceived as embodying the values that are sought to fill that need. It is therefore essential that they have arrived at a personal credo and are able to articulate their managerial philosophy, which will guide their actions through turbulent times.

James M. Kouzes and Barry Z. Posner suggest that leaders cannot lead others until they have first led themselves through a struggle with opposing values. When leaders clarify the principles that will govern their lives and the ends that they will seek, they give purpose to their daily decisions. An ethical set of standards gives a point of reference for navigating the sometimes stormy seas of organizational life. It guides choices of action regardless of the situation and communicates personal integrity that is essential to believability and trust.[3]

Today's libraries seek leaders who have successfully mastered the major developmental phases of adult life and are aware of their own strengths and weaknesses. Such self-awareness provides them with an understanding and empathy for others and promotes tolerance for individual differences. Leader acceptance of self and others creates an environment where experimentation and risk taking can occur, releasing organizational and individual energy that can be directed to achieve changing organizational goals.

Building Trust

Leaders who want to inspire a new organizational vision must be able to create and sustain a trust relationship with their employees and the environment they serve. Building trust is a time-consuming task, especially in today's organizational climate where cynicism, hopelessness, and skepticism of authority abound. Required are courage, faith, patience, and an understanding that without it, the change process cannot be successful. A trust relationship between leaders and followers will provide the framework within which new behaviors can be practiced, risk taking can occur, and failure will not be punished. It will primarily result from the communication of moral goals and the establishment of ethical behavior patters. These need to be consistent with the personal credo of a library's leaders and meet the needs of the organization and its employees. Envisioned and expected are goals similar to the four which John W. Gardner viewed as essential for responsible leadership:

1. Releasing human potential;
2. Balancing the needs of the individual and the community;
3. Defending the fundamental values of the community; and
4. Instilling in individuals a sense of initiative and responsibility.[4]

During the process of creating a trust relationship within a library, leaders need to be highly accessible to and be able to communicate with staff at all levels. They will be called upon over and over to clarify their vision, to explain the underlying philosophy, to model behaviors consistent with the vision, and to defend the beliefs that guide their actions.

Using images with which the employees can identify, speaking their language, expressing their needs, and articulating their dreams will enlist support and create a sense of oneness. This kind of communication is vital to the creation of an organizational culture because it explains and reinforces desired practices, attitudes, and philosophies.

When establishing a trust relationship with their parent institutions, library leaders need to take into consideration that the environment that provides inputs for their organizations is not the same as the environment that receives output. Rather the library functions in what Joanne R. Euster calls a two-environment open system. In such a system the control environment (e.g., a university administration or a city government) grants budgets, but the users make their needs known directly to the library.[5] It is critical for a library leader in changing organizations to persuade the control environment of the necessity to adapt, to alter mission and goals, and to receive funding for valid services or forms of information resources requested by patrons. This separation of the control environment from the user environment often leaves library leaders without strong power bases and increases their need for credibility, trust, and persuasion in order to substantiate their need for sparse resources. Library leaders often have to sell intangible benefits in a very competitive environment. If the need is for automation, for instance, libraries are now competing with all other city and university divisions and departments and are at a disadvantage since cost and benefits are difficult to establish for information access. A library leader may therefore choose to include the need for increased automation in his or her vision to become the best library in the region or state and sell the prestige and status this will bring to the parent institution.

Developing an Organizational History

Before a library administrator can accurately formulate a new organizational vision, he or she must develop an organizational history and analyze its core values. Every organization has an existing culture, and libraries are no exception. It consists of formal and informal policies, modes of interactions, significant historical events, outstanding individuals, traditions, common expectations and values. It provides cohesiveness and a sense of belonging and facilitates understanding, communication, and problem solving.

Analyzing and articulating a library's history build a common linkage among members. In particular, library leaders need to listen to and repeat significant anecdotes, interview key players, meet with staff members of all levels, and analyze their interpretations of the past. Existing core values and important historical figures and events will emerge. These will be different for each institution and may be expressed as adherence to a strong work ethic, pride in the quality of reference service, accuracy in cataloging, being part of an outstanding research university or network, viewing the library staff as one's extended family, building excellent special collections, employing professionally active staff, or having a renowned library director, to name a few. By articulating these values and repeating them in advertisements for vacant positions, interviews of potential staff, orientation programs, brochures, newsletters, and casual and formal conversations, a sense of organizational history can be developed and managed. The history will not only provide the foundation on which the new vision is built, but also communicate respect for the past. It is important to choose carefully those accomplishments and achievements that reinforce newly emerging expectations of excellence.

Creating a Vision

"A vision is the force that invents the future. Leaders spend considerable effort gazing across the horizon of time, imagining what it will be like when they have arrived at their final destination."[6] Today's libraries are in need of visionary leaders who can communicate a need for change and inspire employees to create fresh and exciting possibilities for themselves and the organizations they serve. These leaders are pioneers who are not afraid to seek challenges, take risks, and experiment in order to find better ways of doing things. They will clarify conflicting demands, values, and goals. They need to have the courage to confront conflict, use it, shape it, and mediate it. Above all they must communicate enthusiasm for a better future and make their employees believe that they have the ability to realize that future. To enable them to create support for their vision, these leaders must know the aspirations, dreams, and hopes of their staffs and instill in them confidence that they have the capabilities to realize them. Visionary leaders create causes in which people can believe and that transcend their self-interests. Communicating such a vision requires enthusiasm and passion. An excellent example of a powerful vision was President Kennedy's announcement that the United States was going to send a man to the moon by the end of the 1960s. Before he could make such an announcement, he needed to be sure that it was technologically possible to pursue such a goal. In addition, he needed to be certain that it would appeal to the values of the American public and that the possible sacrifices demanded by the implementation of such a vision would be supported.

Implementing Change: Empowering Others

"Leaders do not achieve success by themselves. Exemplary leaders enlist the support and assistance of all those who must make the project work. They involve, in some ways, those who must live with the results and they make it possible for others to do good work. They encourage collaboration, build teams and empower others. They enable others to act."[7]

How can a library leader enable others to act, to let go of old expectations, tear down comfortable, but inadequate structures, take risks, experiment with new approaches, and create new patterns for serving their constituents? Traditionally libraries achieved their goals through a hierarchical arrangement of divisions and departments with formal communication flowing primarily from the top down. These organizational structures are no longer supportive of the emerging functions and programs, which are created by computerization and demanded by information proliferation, staff, and user expectations.

Effective library leaders will have to examine work flows, environments, positions, job requirements, and tasks and find better structures and means to enable all employees to contribute their talents toward solving complex organizational problems. In the course of assessing a library's history, a new leader will find that most employees will express their expectations for and support of new managerial practices. While everybody needs to be given the opportunity to prove their commitment to organizational changes, it will be essential to the success of organizational change to identify those who are committed to the change process as opposed to those who merely state their support. Recognizing those who agree with the vision and empowering them to act will communicate a serious commitment to change and reinforce their willingness to model the desired behaviors. For example, in libraries with long-term autocratic directors, the employees in formal leadership roles will usually reflect the leadership style of the director. They will generally agree with the director, expect strong directives, appear passive and acquiescent toward their superiors while exhibiting autocratic behaviors toward their subordinates. They can be expected to support the hierarchical organizational structures and communication channels.

Such organizations also have very strong informal organizational leaders, who have organized work flow, maintained group cohesiveness, encouraged lateral communication, provided emotional support to individuals, and evaluated the effectiveness of services and managers. These informal leaders usually yield a great deal of power based on their competencies and personality traits, but they have never achieved the formal recognition and authority that goes with that power. A new library director who wants to create a more participative environment may start by recognizing the competencies of these informal leaders, formalizing their authority through promotions into positions of power, and soliciting their help in communicating the new core values associated with participative management. As Herbert S. White points out, "It makes perfectly good sense to notice natural leaders within a library and groom them for management promotions."[8] Libraries that embrace errors and encourage risk taking will provide the environment necessary for leaders and managers to implement the vision of change.

The promotion of such natural leaders into positions of power will signal to all employees that expertise will be rewarded in the future. Because their power is based on competence and the good will of those who perform the daily tasks, promoting these leaders will substantially increase upward and lateral communication within the organization. This assures that the new values are disseminated widely and reinforced by the formal and informal organization. It will result in increased contact between organizational levels and facilitate the sharing of ideas and information.

To further reward excellence at all levels, library leaders may want to institute upward evaluations to signal to the staff that the same performance expectations are in effect for all and that staff perceptions and insights are important in organizational decision making. Too many administrators and leaders have never asked for employee feedback on their performance, because it is very risky. Instituting such evaluations can greatly improve communication throughout the library because the staff realize and appreciate the trust exhibited in their judgment. Significant discrepancies in perception about supervisors' or managers' performance can be used to clarify organizational or departmental expectations or recommend continuing education.

Staff Development Programs

With power comes responsibility, and visionary library leaders know that they need to provide opportunities for all employees to acquire those competencies necessary to participate in creating and sustaining new cultures and organizations. The funding of staff-development programs communicates strongly that the new organizational culture values its employees and is willing to invest in their future. In addition, enlightened library leaders recognize that training sessions, topics selected, and trainers can serve as powerful tools for communicating new organizational values.

While most library employees are highly intelligent and educated, their supervisory and communication skills are often sadly lacking. In addition to these basic managerial competencies, the complexity of today's organizations and the change process require that both leaders and employees acquire or refresh their knowledge about organizational development, participative management skills, and the nature and distribution of power in order to anticipate problems and to create common frames of reference.

While all employees may believe, for example, that they should be involved in the decision-making processes of their institutions, they may initially lack the courage or maturity to assume the consequences for the outcome of their decisions. Employees often exhibit a lack of understanding of the limits of their potential involvement caused by the real constraints of their positions, education, training, or the organization's resources. Participative management does not mean that everybody is involved in all organizational decisions and has equal access to power. Rather, it means that those employees who are affected by a particular decision and who have to implement that decision should be involved in making that decision and should have sufficient power to implement it. Too many employees falsely believe that everything is their business and waste much organizational energy and effort in meddling in other departments' affairs. Communicating these differences takes time, trial and error, and much tact. It is the responsibility of leaders in evolving libraries to constantly define and redefine issues, listen to concerns, and explain limits.

The initial sharing of organizational power will create a high level of expectation among employees who have never had access to it. The positive feeling of using power to achieve goals and recognition invariably creates a need for more. In changing libraries, leaders must artfully share their power appropriately without raising unrealistic expectations and discouraging initiative. Staff-development seminars can also be used to provide a common intellectual basis for understanding and discussing those larger managerial issues, which will be new to most employees. They may help to prevent some misunderstandings and misinterpretations of emerging organizational roles and responsibilities.

Sustaining Organizational Progress

It is inevitable that library employees become tired, disenchanted, frustrated, and stressed during the lengthy and arduous change process. To prevent disillusionment, leaders must continue to act as the organizational role model and create reward systems that celebrate milestones and reinforce positive contributions toward the new organizational culture. They need to recognize individual excellence and group contributions in meetings, through staff-recognition programs, and in articles in newsletters and other publications in order to encourage a continuation of efforts. In addition, recruitment and orientation of new staff members with compatible values will sustain the change momentum, while those who cannot support the new managerial direction can be assisted with career counseling to find more compatible work environments.

Role Modeling

As organizational frustrations increase, role modeling becomes more important. Both supporters and detractors of the change process will try to detect inconsistencies between words and deeds to justify their own behavior. "A leader's words and deeds must not only be internally consistent, but they must also coordinate with, support, or reinforce the new organizational ideals. They must match what the organization considers the epitome of desired behavior."[9]

Being a role model takes vigilance. Leaders must act consistently with the values they espouse, according to Tom Peters, co-author of *In Search of Excellence*. To do so takes consistency, persistence, and attention to detail. Role modeling requires that one's values are clear and internalized so that decisions and actions can flow naturally, without much deliberation. Nothing loses the respect of staff as fast as inconsistencies between words and deeds.

Reward Systems

Carefully designed and implemented reward systems are excellent communication tools to reinforce the practice of new procedures, policies, and values. Effective library leaders must first communicate clearly which behaviors will be rewarded and then administer the reward fairly and consistently. While most libraries suffer from a lack of financial resources to recognize excellence, the use of nonfinancial recognition is limited only by a leader's creativity. Such recognition can range from the proverbial "pat-on-the-back" and thank-you notes, to public recognition through staff-appreciation programs, excellence awards, and articles in library publications.

Of equal importance as the rewarding of desired behaviors are the identification and extinguishing of undesirable behaviors, mainly through withholding approval or recognition.

Recruiting and Orientation

When instituting a new organizational culture, the recruitment and orientation of new staff members are important opportunities to reinforce core values. The higher the level of the vacant position, the more important becomes the fit between individual and organizational values. Using search committees to screen potential candidates for their suitability to a changing library environment helps employees to articulate the organizational core values. It also requires them to decide during the search process whether they want to be a part of the organization that they are "selling" to candidates. Most employees will not feel comfortable on search committees if they do not agree with the library's new mission. If disagreements between individual belief systems and organizational values cannot be resolved, the employee will likely start looking for a library with values similar to his or her own.

The more succinctly the emerging culture is communicated before and during the interview process, the better the chances that a match between candidate and library can be achieved. If organizational expectations are clearly understood, the orientation process can then be used to integrate and socialize a new employee into the system. Formal orientations can present the factual data about the library, its history, functions, and greater environment, while mentors and trainers can teach and explain the underlying philosophy and values of the library through daily contacts and informal means like friendships and conversations during coffee breaks and lunches.

Career Counseling

Changes in organizational cultures will create many stresses and anxieties for long-time employees because the expectations and rules under which they functioned are losing validity. If they support the emerging culture, they will likely seek to play an active part in its creation and grow with the opportunities presented. Fostering the careers of those who support new directions gives library leaders another opportunity to reward commitment to change with more influence. Inside promotions give powerful signals of what attitudes, skills, and behaviors are valued because the persons are already well known and usually yield substantial informal power.

Those who are unable to support the new directions will require special attention and patience. Dealing with them fairly and giving them the time and the opportunity to change will signal to all employees that the library leader understands the difficulties inherent in the change process and proves his or her tolerance of individual differences. If it still becomes necessary to help an employee leave the organization, the decision will be supported because the staff know that every effort has been made to assist that person to adjust to clearly communicated expectations. This is especially true if the majority of employees have become supportive of change and a reasonable time period has elapsed for the staff to be knowledgeable about desirable behaviors. Should an employee be unable or unwilling to integrate himself or herself into the new culture, it will be helpful to use career counseling, out-placement, and other assistance to facilitate his or her separation. All these measures will attest to a leader's serious commitment to enlightened human-resources practices and encourage risk taking by those who prove more adaptable within the organization.

Conclusion

Libraries are changing and need strong leadership to create adaptable organizations and involve employees in the management process. Leaders in libraries will have to communicate new directions during uncertain times. They must possess the skills to implement new organizational and programmatic changes and build the same skills in their staffs. As spokespersons of the organization, they will be required to persuade their funding authorities, users, and staffs that the envisioned changes will better serve their needs. They will have to communicate their commitment to change not only through words, but through sustained actions.

References

1. Joanne R. Euster, "Leaders and Managers: Literature Review, Synthesis and a New Conceptual Framework," *Journal of Library Administration* 5 (Spring 1984): 55.
2. Ibid., 56
3. James M. Kouzes and Barry Z. Posner, *The Leadership Challenge: How to Get Extraordinary Things Done in Organizations* (San Francisco: Jossey-Bass, 1987), 300–301.
4. John W. Gardner, *The Moral Aspect of Leadership: Leadership Papers/5* (Washington, D.C.: Independent Sector, 1987), 14.
5. Euster, "Leaders and Managers," 57–58.
6. Kouzes and Posner, *Leadership Challenge*, 10.
7. Ibid.
8. Herbert White, "Oh, Where Have All the Leaders Gone?" *Library Journal* (October 1, 1987): 69.
9. Bruce McAfee and Betty J. Ricks, "Leadership by Example: Do As I Do!" *Management Solutions* 31 (August 1986): 16.

14

Creative Library Leadership for the 1990s: Using Team Management to Ensure Two-Way Communication in an Academic Library

HANNELORE B. RADER

Using creative approaches to problem solving in an academic library setting is an idea whose time has come. Newly developed technologies are helping to improve library work and services, and innovative solutions to problems are a must because traditional models are no longer effective.

Creative managers can guide their staffs toward a path of innovative problem solving and prepare them for the risk taking implied in that. Such managers must be able to assess traditional situations with a view to the future and initiate appropriate changes. They must become change agents within their library and role models for their staffs. They must be able to seize opportunities and develop them in innovative ways for the express purpose of providing users with the best and most effective library service. Creative managers will approach situations positively and will be successful in taking advantage of opportunities whenever they present themselves.

As the information age develops and change will be a constant, innovative organizations featuring effective communication will have to be developed for the twenty-first century. Managers will have to be adept at creating flexible work environments to address developing challenges.

To ensure that libraries develop into dynamic information centers where knowledge can be actively explored, tested, enlarged, and developed by the academic community, innovative approaches to managing the library organization will be mandatory.

Need for New Organizational Structure

To address successfully the changes brought about by new technologies, new organizational structures need to be developed in academic libraries. Although libraries share several common characteristics with other types of organizations, they are different in some ways. They are service agencies for information, not profit-making organizations. They perform functions both of supply and guidance, the latter without the benefit of a personal and continuous client relationship. Currently, libraries do not have clear-cut objectives because they have accumulated functions and methodologies that make for rigid structure and resistance to change. At the same time, information needs and demands are becoming more urgent as well as expensive, marketable commodities. Libraries are subjected to pressures from faculties, users, and political groups and face tremendous challenges related to new information formats, extraordinary high-cost inflation, and user demand for more timely information delivery.

There are certain givens for the libraries of the twenty-first century. Libraries will remain a major source of scholarly and scientific information, but they will provide that information through new technologies. The latter will make them a major part of the campus computer network and thus an integral part of a complex information system. Such a system will need improved strategic planning based on evaluation of cost and performance. Resource sharing will become more important and complex. More and better studies will be needed to assess quality of service, alternative publication in libraries, and the effect of use fees and pricing policies on library economics.

Library Leadership Challenge

Much of the management literature laments the fact that it is difficult to be an effective leader at this time. Employees tend to question the authority of leaders more than ever. Today's leader must be able to inspire confidence and trust in employees; traditional leadership is not well suited for today's organization.

Library managers must deal with challenges related to leadership as well as changing methodologies to provide scholars with necessary information. They must find the appropriate place for the library within an automated campus and within the planning process in higher education, particularly as related to resource allocations. The latter involves decision making related to who pays for what. Today's library leader must be able to predict changes produced by the introduction of new technologies, must develop methods to measure the cost effectiveness of library performance, and must be able to adapt the library to the institution's changing goals and objectives.

Similarly, present library leaders must build analytical and technical skills within library staffs so that they can handle expert systems derived from artificial intelligence research. They must use performance measures and accounting tools as a basis for program planning and fit the library into the overall institutional environment. They must become astute politicians to share effectively the ever-shrinking resources available for higher education. They must become change agents for the faculty and students to help them utilize new information technologies effectively within the curricula and to continue the evaluation of information while fighting censorship and promoting preservation of rapidly deteriorating materials.

Taking into consideration the many individual differences within a given library staff, the various personal needs of each employee, the different value systems of individuals, and the concept of human dignity, library leaders will certainly be challenged. They must build an effective and capable work force for newly automated library processes. They will need to consider integration of library functions and employ library personnel with computer and technical expertise.

The Team Approach to Library Management

Team leadership accomplishes work through commitment in a climate of trust and respect. Interdependency is achieved through a common stake in organizational purpose.

Members of a mature management team know their own and others' tasks well enough so that nothing falls through the cracks; they know who should be performing which functions.

Trust is so high that the group does not need to meet on every issue; all members know, and are committed to, the same goals and know each other's attitudes and positions on issues. Any member can act in the department's name when necessary, without seeking everybody's approval. Each member is confident that no one, including the boss, acts without consultation unless there is a good reason—such as prior general agreement, special expertise, legitimate time pressures, or unavailability of affected parties; and the person who does act knows that others would back any action.

Such a group is not very "groupy," or clinging, and does not waste time meeting on trivial issues or limiting those who have taken individual initiative. A lot of individual work is assigned to be done outside meetings, with reports and recommendations brought back to the team. Members who are clearly more expert than others in certain areas are given great latitude to make the decisions on those matters.

When issues affect several areas of the department as a whole, however, members seriously address the issues together, fight hard and openly for their beliefs, insist that their concerns be addressed, and yet also pay attention to the needs of the department as a whole. Everyone is comfortable wearing at least two hats, one for his or her area and one for the department.

Although skilled at persuasion and willing to fight hard over important differences, members feel no obligation to oppose automatically initiatives from other members or the manager. There is no competition for competition's sake. Members would enthusiastically support the positions or ideas of others with which they happened to agree; furthermore, when they are in opposition to one another, the battles center on issues, not personalities. Differences are considered legitimate expressions of a person's experiences and job perspective, not indications of incompetence, stupidity, or political maneuvering.

Despite members' willingness to fight when necessary, the climate is pervasively supportive, encouraging members to ask one another for help, acknowledge their mistakes, share resources (people, information, or equipment), and generally further everybody's performance and learning.

The group pays attention to successful task achievement and to individual members' learning; members are not restricted to areas where they have total competence and hence cannot acquire new expertise, nor are they so overloaded with learning experiences that group performance seriously suffers. Cautious members are pushed to venture into less secure areas, while overreaching members are reminded that new opportunities cannot supplant ongoing responsibilities.

Perhaps most important, the group has self-correcting mechanisms; when things are not going well, all members are ready to examine the group's processes, discuss what is wrong, and take corrective action. Whatever the problems—overly lengthy meetings, inappropriate agenda items, unclear responsibilities, lack of team effort, overly parochial participation, or even poor leadership practices—the group takes time out to assess its way of operating and to make midcourse corrections. Individual members, as well as the manager, feel free to raise questions of team performance, but the group is not so overly self-analyzing that it neglects its main tasks. High task performance remains a central concern.

To build an effective team the manager must have the skills and intention to develop a team approach and allocate time to appropriate team-building activities. Management becomes somewhat of a shared function by allowing other members who have the skills needed by the team to exercise leadership when appropriate. Members of the team must be qualified and capable of contributing to a variety of needs to create the needed balance. Team members should feel a sense of commitment to the aims and purposes of the team. They must be willing to devote personal energy to building the team and supporting other team members. The team must develop a climate in which individuals can relax, be open and direct, and are prepared to take risks. Objectives of the team must be clearly understood by all and must be felt to be worthwhile. The team's energy is devoted to achieving results, and team members' performance is reviewed frequently so that improvements can be made. The team contributes to library planning and plays a productive role in the organization. Effective problem solving has to be developed by the entire team.

Roles of the team and its members are clearly defined. Communication patterns are well developed and administrative procedures support a team approach. Mistakes and weaknesses are studied without personal attack so that the group can learn together from these experiences. The team needs members who can make strong individual contributions. Creativity of the team is at its peak through interaction from new ideas and innovative risk taking that is rewarded. Good ideas are translated into action.

Relationships with other teams are systematically developed to provide open communications and to allow for more productive results. Regular contact and review of joint priorities occur on a regular basis. Individuals are encouraged to work with members of other teams.

Several cautions that have to do with the various stages through which any team progresses need to be considered when implementing the team-management concept. The first phase is an orientation period and is marked by much excitement. The second phase is marked by dissatisfaction of team members, things may not work too well at first because individuals are not yet ready to cooperate as fully as they must for effective team work.

The third phase is one in which solutions to problems are found cooperatively and the team becomes more cohesive. The last phase is the actual production period when the team begins to perform in a cooperative manner. Time and patience are needed on the part of the manager to get through these four phases.

Furthermore, it is important that the manager chooses team members wisely. Any team should include individuals with various skills in the area of organization, production, creativity, and problem solving.

Communication

Successful communication skills are critical prerequisites for managers since organization activities are unified through the communication process. If communication is poor, the entire organization suffers and the manager is in trouble. Communication occurs orally, in written format, and nonverbally and also includes listening skills.

Oral communication can be on an individual basis or in groups. It is important for managers to ensure that team members hear and understand them by having someone else summarize what they have said.

Written communication is a more formal way of stating a message in memos, letters, reports, policies, and procedures. It takes training and skill to write clear and unambiguous communications. Nonverbal communication involves body language and is often difficult to control; nonverbal behavior can easily contradict a verbal communication.

Organizational communication can influence employees' motivation a great deal if one considers information's power. Individuals often measure their status in the organization by the kind of information they receive. Effective communication occurs in a nonthreatening atmosphere, is honest and direct, and includes an element of trust. It is planned and prepared well. It utilizes direct feedback and involves good listening skills.

A skillful manager will be able to effectively use the formal, informal, and any external communication system by understanding each one and being able to determine which system to use in what situation.

A New Urban University Library Model

At Cleveland State University, problem solving is being approached creatively. A new organizational structure (fig. 1) of the library was implemented in August 1987.

The new organizational structure of CSU Libraries features a blending of services and a softening of area demarcations to accommodate the automation of all services. The structure features collection management, information services, document-delivery services, bibliographic services, and administrative services; staff responsibility crossovers exist. Managers function in a participatory environment that utilizes teams and other action groups to address problems and issues in creative ways.

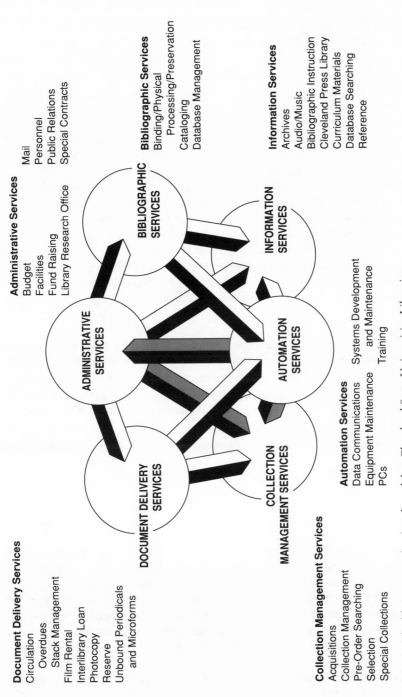

Document Delivery Services
Circulation
Overdues
Stack Management
Film Rental
Interlibrary Loan
Photocopy
Reserve
Unbound Periodicals
and Microforms

Collection Management Services
Acquisitions
Collection Management
Pre-Order Searching
Selection
Special Collections

Automation Services
Data Communications
Equipment Maintenance
PCs
Systems Development
and Maintenance
Training

Administrative Services
Budget
Facilities
Fund Raising
Library Research Office
Mail
Personnel
Public Relations
Special Contracts

Bibliographic Services
Binding/Physical
Processing/Preservation
Cataloging
Database Management

Information Services
Archives
Audio/Music
Bibliographic Instruction
Cleveland Press Library
Curriculum Materials
Database Searching
Reference

Fig. 1. The library organizational model at Cleveland State Universities Libraries

Within administrative services an Office of Library Studies and Research was established with an ambitious agenda. This office provides grant support for the library, bibliographic research support for grant-related and special faculty projects, research help for the campus development office, statistical development for the library, and evaluation studies of library services and collections. It is staffed by the most experienced senior library faculty member.

New relationships and services are being developed with the urban community to help the campus with recruitment and retention of minorities. Library internships for inner-city high school students and an innovative reference-assistant program are but the beginnings of that endeavor. The library is playing a more active role in supporting campus concerns regarding minority student recruitment and retention.

Friends of the Library has been resurrected and is aggressively pursuing a major publicity and marketing program for the library to inform the campus and urban community about library services. Programs on the horizon feature special collections and special talents both with the faculty and the community and promise exciting years ahead. This group is also helping to position the library within the developmental affairs of the university, which are just beginning to take off.

Overall, it seems that Cleveland State University Libraries's agenda for innovative services and projects is growing at an accelerated pace. New opportunities are presenting themselves faster than we are able to deal with them. Once an organization decides to "go creative" and people understand what that means, there are virtually no limits for growth and success.

Development of the New Organization

The new organization has already progressed through various steps of development in its first eight months. These stages parallel closely the development of team management.

Phase one lasted a little over a month. It began with the introduction of the new organizational structure to the staff and produced excitement as well as anxiety. The new structure had been planned for five months with solicited information from staff members, a consultant, and appropriate research by the director. A management team was selected by the director, and the structure was finalized at a management team retreat. A few days before the new organizational structure was presented to the entire staff, a festive commemorative social event was held for the library staff to honor past accomplishments by the staff and begin a tradition for this relatively new institution.

Implementation began the morning after the staff meeting in which the new structure was presented. Major shifts in personnel and locations had to be handled. Many staff members needed much training for new responsibilities. Policies and procedures had to be revised and developed. Anxieties and fears had to be addressed, and all that while continuing an excellent service record and preparing for a new fall quarter.

During this period the library staff was also involved in planning for and selecting a library automation system, together with staff members from the law library and the computer services department. These three groups had never worked together, let alone on a project of such universal proportions and implications for the future. It must be pointed out that the staff completed this enormous task—involving eighty people working together with faculty input to select an automation system for the library—in a period of eight months.

Needless to say, this was a hectic, often almost chaotic, time. The management team was under enormous stress, particularly since most of them were new to management of this type and in this format. The team held marathon sessions, often ten or more hours a week.

Phase two came quickly. Almost everyone became upset and dissatisfied. Staff did not get training quickly enough to handle new responsibilities; some responsibilities fell into cracks, thus creating emergency situations. There was much mistrust of the management team and communication seemed at an all-time low. Perceptions of the new organization and the management team were mostly negative. In addition, money for student help was tight and some vacancies could not be filled quickly, creating more pressures for the already hard-working staff.

It is to the staff's credit that they were creative and certainly not timid. At first they vented their frustrations through an underground newsletter, a parody of an existing weekly library newsletter, which is used to communicate with the staff and was obviously not fulfilling this purpose at that time. The underground newsletter , hardly flattering to the management, communicated to the management that something was definitely wrong. Four months into phase two, a staff meeting was held to assess the new organization and its problems. Everyone voiced his or her opinions and perceptions in a brainstorming session. The emerging issues were put into priority order, and the top three were elected, and followed by another brainstorming session on solving these problems. The management team then took these issues and began to address them; this was the beginning of phase three.

In phase three the management team began developing solutions to problems while becoming more cohesive as a team. Meetings became more efficient and organized. The three major issues that were addressed were decision making, communication, and distrust. Although we are still in phase three, good progress is being made toward the fourth and final phase when effective cooperation will produce positive results. Time and patience have paid off so far.

It is important to point out that the three issues that were addressed in the third phase—decision making, distrust, and communication—are crucial to the success of the new organizational structure and team management.

Decision Making

Decision making in a team-management setting is very different from decision making in an autocratic or hierarchical structure. At first, decision making in a group setting seems most uncomfortable, cumbersome, and certainly confusing. The management team spent much time and energy in developing principles of decision making for the library and decided the team involved in decision making would be as follows:

Decisions about operations are made as close to the operation as possible.

Decisions affecting more than one unit are made by the services head.

Decisions affecting more than one service are referred to the management team for decisions by the director. In the event of a question, the matter should be referred to the management team.

Decisions about engaging in new projects, directions, and services are made by the director.

Decisions affecting budget, personnel, policy, and facilities are made by the director, or are delegated.

The director, deputy director, and services heads can create teams. Unless specifically empowered by a management team member, teams do not make decisions but contribute to decision making through making appropriate recommendations.

This task was difficult for the management team, and the application of these principles is still being tested. Throughout their discussions, team members kept in mind that an effective decision requires access to all facts of the situation, being aware of various perceptions of the situation, exploring various solutions, and planning the implementation activities of the decision and analyzing possible alternatives. Team members became aware of various barriers that affect decision making as well. These barriers include differences in perception, fear of the consequences and of failure, conflicting loyalties, failure to base a decision on an evaluation of the situation, and inflexibility.

Distrust

The management team knew from the beginning that there was much distrust of them on the part of the staff, particularly because of the history of library management and partially because of having to deal with a totally new and unknown management as well as a new structure. They were also aware of the fact that building trust would not happen quickly and would take much patience and attention. Several projects assisted with the development of trust. Examples included: the development of performance standards by a staff team, planning exhibits as a team, and using the team approach for resolving collection-development issues. Most of all, however, it was the management team's weekly meetings that worried the staff. To solve this problem the management team first decided to bring in various staff members for reports and then broadened the decision to include a different staff member each week. In addition, a secretary was assigned to take the minutes instead of a member of the team. Furthermore, it was decided to base performance evaluations on performance standards. New and revised job descriptions are discussed more widely, and creative problem solving is encouraged. Already several staff members have proposed and implemented several money-saving mechanisms.

Communication

Overall, it is really communication that is often the cause of most organizational problems, including decision making and distrust. Perceptions of what is going on, often not based on reality, create many problem situations. The management team must continually monitor and improve their communication skills. They must above all become good listeners and provide direct and honest information to staff members. They must be confident, nonthreatening and unemotional whenever possible. All of them are working on this very difficult task. Everyone has certain personality traits that can interfere with being an excellent communicator. Training and education are provided for anyone who seeks to improve his or her communication skills. Members of all teams are encouraged to practice at all times the communication skills outlined and to use summaries and feedback mechanisms as part of their communication techniques.

Management-team members are heads of their service areas and as such have to be effective leaders and communicators for the library management as well as the staff. This is not an easy task. Each one has a different style and modus operandi, yet the communications must be similar or the organization will be in trouble. Some progress has been made in this direction, but much more is needed.

Conclusion

Is the new organization appropriate for the needs of Cleveland State University Libraries? Was team management a good approach to take? These are the questions that the library management is asking. The answer to these questions is a definite yes, although the first year of the new organization was most challenging for the library leadership. The agenda was a bit too ambitious and too many changes were instituted the initial year.

However, it was the right thing to do given the existing circumstances. Many challenges have been and will have to be addressed. The library staff was successful in gaining faculty and administrative support for increasing the library materials budget. Half of the library offices have been automated, and the other half will become automated shortly. Staff members are becoming very knowledgeable in using microcomputers for their operations. A library automation system for Cleveland State University Libraries and the CSU Law Library is being implemented without additional staff.

There are many projects for the next year, and much will be accomplished because the staff is slowly becoming a team. This lengthy process takes patience, but the results are worth it. Staff members are gaining new skills in holding meetings in communicating, problem solving, critical thinking, and taking risks. Creative abilities of all staff are surfacing and helping to address important issues successfully. Continued patience and much learning will help the staff to strengthen the team management concept.

Finally, a flexible organization coupled with a team approach to solving problems is the only one that will help libraries to remain in the mainstream of the evolving information society.

15

Communication as Essential for Leadership to a Public Good: An Information Infrastructure

ROBERT F. MORAN, JR.

Consistent with the calling of professionals, librarians have concerns that reach beyond the limits of their work. The agenda of the ALA Council provides adequate proof of their interest in issues that reach beyond librarianship. Equal treatment for minorities and education reform are but two of the issues librarians have spoken on and actively pursued. The conception of librarians as leaders, then, cannot be limited to leadership within the library. Effective leadership is equally important when librarians seek to influence those outside the profession.

Leadership frequently seems to be considered, or at least written about,[1] as a quality of a particular kind of person. A set of traits (the ability to envision, to communicate, to motivate) is used to describe this person. She or he is different from the others whom the leader takes above and beyond generally accepted objectives. Yet there is nothing about leadership that denies it to those in whom leadership traits do not predominate (i.e., many who may not be perceived as leaders can lead from time to time).

Leadership is defined as the ability to recognize a goal unknown to a group of people yet of significance to them, and then, to influence the group to strive for the goal. It assumes that a broad range of people are capable of acting in this manner at times, so that most librarians can be looked to for leadership. Focusing on leadership outside the profession, it suggests that an opportunity for this leadership exists in the convergence of libraries and computer centers. In describing this opportunity and what is needed to take advantage of it, the central role of communication in leadership will be demonstrated.

A Call to Lead

The report *Freedom and Equality of Access to Information* calls for librarians to lead toward several objectives that will contribute to broad access to information.[2] Among these is the creation of an information infrastructure encompassing traditional information fields and the newer electronically based enterprises. The report implies that the public good has been and continues to be served through formal and informal communication among the producers and users of print products and states that these relationships must be duplicated with those who provide information in electronic forms:

> the availability of printed materials to the American public . . . requires an enormous complex and interrelated institutional structure, including authors, publishers, magazine and newspaper distributors, book wholesalers and sellers, book clubs, mail order services, and libraries. These are linked by impressive cataloging and bibliographic services and interlibrary loan and cooperative practices that have been built up over the decades. They permit the inquirer . . . to identify, locate, and usually gain access to any text desired from among the tens of millions that exist. If we are to be able to take similar advantage of the powerful new technologies becoming available to us, we will need to create a comparable institutional structure, linked by comparable bibliographic standards and comparable cooperative practices.[3]

The Library Administration and Management Association (LAMA) task force charged to study and respond to the access report committed LAMA to lead in the creation of this information infrastructure. It recommends that LAMA assume

> a leadership role in the library and information community to define and help establish the information infrastructure that will support our society in the near future. Important patterns of communication and cooperation for the public good among producers and acquirers (including libraries) of print products have not been established among producers

and acquirers in the electronic marketplace. LAMA should assist its individual members in the American Library Association in creating this infrastructure by taking a leadership role now.[4]

Earlier in its report, the LAMA task force perceptively notes that librarians, for a number of years, have known and considered the problems with which the access report dealt. Continuing, the task force states, "We are, however, coming up short of concrete objectives that could move us toward correction in improvement in many of these areas."[5] To put the task force's observation in more general terms, high-sounding goals frequently go unmet for lack of leadership and a practical means for their attainment.

An opportunity and practical means to lead toward the creation of an information infrastructure exists in the convergence of libraries and computer centers. Computer center employees, as members of the computer and electronics industry, can both serve as conduits for messages from outside the industry and also influence decision making within it. That is, if librarians can enlist the support of these people in developing relationships between more traditional information producers and deliverers and electronic publishers, a contribution toward broadening the information infrastructure will have been made.

Convergence of Libraries and Computer Centers

The movement of computer centers and libraries toward each other within colleges has been documented. The merger of the library and academic computer center at Columbia University is known to most.[6] In addition, Douglas E. Van Houweling observed that "the convergence of university library operations and the university's computer resources is already becoming obvious at most universities."[7] Also, Richard M. Dougherty considers the growing relationship between campus libraries and computer centers and, after stating his belief that the merger of these two units is unlikely, agrees that they will be closely related.[8]

This stronger and closer relationship between libraries and computer centers is likely to develop within schools and organizations with special libraries. Though evidence for this is not as available as for colleges, it is reasonable to suggest that it is occurring, or, at least, will occur, because of the similarities of the activities performed by libraries and computer centers. For example, computers are information processing machines, a fact evident by their adoption by libraries. In addition, computer centers are moving to provide direct access to information stores just as libraries do.

For instance, computer centers purchase machine-readable data sources and provide these to their users. Computer centers also connect their users with off-site databases just as librarians are connecting their users with bibliographic databases. Finally, libraries and computer centers are generally support services providing assistance to the primary functions of their organizations.

Since public libraries are more autonomous than college, school, and special libraries, this convergence is less likely and the relationship between the library and the local government's computing agency may not be as close as that in the other areas. Still, the use of computers by public libraries, and the similarities between libraries and computing agencies, will at least provide an opportunity for close relationships that many librarians will use to their advantage.

Librarians, then, can expect to be coming in closer and more frequent contact with the people who are responsible for and knowledgeable about computers. They will deal more with these individuals as colleagues involved in the solution of problems affecting their units. In this way, they will be brought in close contact with the universe of users and producers of information in electronic form. Herein lies the opportunity for librarians not only to influence the computer professionals with whom they work, but also to communicate the goals and values of librarianship to these individuals in their capacities as members of the work force that creates, manufactures, maintains, and operates computer technology.

Leadership through Communication

The convergence of libraries and computer centers presents an opportunity for librarians to communicate with computer center personnel. With regard to the extension of an information infrastructure to electronic publishing, librarians can demonstrate the need for (1) standards for electronically published information; (2) a widely accepted, simple method for identifying these information sources; and (3) a standard method of indexing them. In addition, broader library values can be made known (e.g., quick, straightforward access to information sources no matter where they may be and free or inexpensive access).

Effective Communication

The communications model described by Ronald B. Adler and George Rodman both demonstrates the difficulty of communication in this situation and provides the understanding needed for success.[9] As expected, the model includes a sender, a receiver, a communication channel, and the message. In addition, it recognizes that the communicators are people with unique experiences and attributes, and it includes the interference that always exists when two people attempt to communicate with each other. Finally, by depicting each participant as a sender and a receiver, it illustrates that communication requires that the sender be responsive to the receiver.

In defining "environment" in this communication model, these authors note:

> By this term, we do not mean simply physical location, but also the personal history that each person brings to a conversation. The problem here is that each of us represents a different environment because of our different backgrounds. Although we certainly have some experience in common, we also see the situation in a unique way.[10]

The authors continue by explaining that the effectiveness of communication depends on the overlapping of these environments; successful communication depends on the similarity of the understanding and experiences of the communicators.

In identifying "interference," the model reminds the reader that elements seemingly unrelated to the communication process can hinder or even cause it to be completely ineffective. They term these elements "noise." After noting the existence of physical noise, they define psychological noise as "forces within the sender or receiver that make these people less able to express or understand the message."[11] Negative feelings of one person toward the other, and feelings of fear, aggression, and hostility can give rise to this kind of noise.

Finally, the model shows that the sender must listen. The common perception of communication as primarily an active process is wrong. Successful communication requires more passive response than action, more listening than talking. Listening involves three activities: hearing the spoken message, receiving the nonverbal messages, and verifying that the interpretation of these responses is accurate. The verbal message must be heard accurately and decoded properly; nonverbal messages must be perceived and properly interpreted. In addition, each party to the interaction must periodically check to see that the message is being received accurately. The most common way this is done is by saying, "Is this what you mean?"

The librarian wishing to influence computer center personnel must recognize and be aware of each of the elements in this model. First, the message itself must be a clear one, unencumbered by unnecessary information and clearly understood by the person sending it. Second, the message must be coded in a way that will ensure accurate decoding; words must be used that are meaningful to computer center personnel. Third, an appropriate channel must be chosen. Given the superiority of face-to-face communication (i.e., immediate feedback, the nonverbal component, and the ability to control noise), this channel is probably more appropriate here than written or electronically transmitted words.

Before the message is sent, however, consideration must have been given to the broader aspects of the communication model, the necessity of overlapping sender and receiver environments, and the reduction of noise possibilities. Regarding overlapping environments, it is worth pointing out the extent to which librarians and computer center personnel differ. Despite the suggestion above that similarities between libraries and computer centers will bring the personnel in these organizations together, the differences between the two organizations—and between the personnel in each of the organizations—are more numerous. First, and perhaps the most important, libraries are long-standing organizations with even longer traditions, while computer centers are recent establishments. The organizational climate of a long-established enterprise will differ radically from the newly formed one. On the one hand, organizations that have existed for a long time will have many detailed, tested processes through which organizational goals are met. More recently formed units will, on the other hand, have few of these, and rather, rely on the development of specific methods for meeting specific aims or solving problems as they arise. In the first case, impersonal rules and regulations predominate; in the second, people and their ability to understand the new situation and develop and respond to it will be of more importance. Also, the missions of libraries and computer centers differ in that the former is well defined while the latter is consistently changing in response to new technologies and new opportunities.

In addition, other less basic but more numerous differences exist. Polley A. McClure quotes John R. Sack as writing the following: "Librarians are struggling to incorporate the computer within their long tradition of consistency while computer centers struggle to develop some consistency in a context of constant change." [12] The knowledge and skills bases of librarians derive from professional training in the discipline of librarianship, which is reasonably stable and often incorporates a discipline-specific focus. On the other hand, there is no specific professional training for computer center staff. They usually possess some set of skills in an application or process area, but these are often acquired through experience in some other field. [13] The two organizations have very different traditions of user fees; libraries usually offer their services for no fee, while computer centers usually charge.

Pat Molholt points to other differences between these organizations and the people who populate them. [14] Libraries tend to have a user-friendly orientation, highly structured files and collections, relative uniformity of access that generally requires little user training, and a high degree of subject expertise. Computer centers, on the other hand, have yet to develop fully the user-focused service typical of library reference desks, and their services are frequently more difficult to understand and to use. This list of differences should be sufficient to prove the point: despite the similarities that have resulted in the convergence of some libraries and computer centers, the differences between the organizations and between those who populate them are substantial.

These dissimilarities will, most probably, provide the greatest challenge to a librarian wishing to exercise leadership as the paths of libraries and computer centers come together. Differences in values, perceptions, goals, and behaviors will stand in the way. Thus, the librarian must make a special effort to bring the Adler-Rodman environments into coincidence by understanding computer center personnel and the situations in which they work before attempting to send difficult messages to them.

Continuing a consideration of communication with computer center personnel from the perspective provided by the Adler-Rodman model, the librarian must recognize and deal with the noise and interference that will hinder communication. While physical noise needs to be avoided, psychological noise will be more difficult because, being less obvious, it may not be recognized. Thus, librarians should enter into exchanges with computer center personnel with the understanding that, as people, they share with us uncertainty, a reluctance to change, and a pride in their efforts and achievements.

Finally, the librarian wishing to lead in encounters with computer center personnel must be a listener. Adler and Rodman relate two telling experiments on listening. First, a study of business people demonstrated the significance of this skill: when the time spent speaking, writing, reading, and listening was recorded, it was found that 42 percent of the time was spent listening. Second, a study of the in-class behavior of college students determined that, at randomly chosen times, no more than 12 percent were hearing correctly what the lecturer was saying. [15] These experiments point to the importance of listening and the frequent failure to do it well.

Upon consideration, failures in listening are not surprising. Years are spent learning how to speak, read, and write, while practically no time is spent learning how to listen. And so, particular attention needs to be given to this component of communication. The practices of asking questions (e.g., "What do you mean?") and listening actively (repeating the message in one's own words) both force the listener to pay closer attention and provide the opportunity to verify whether a message has been accurately received.

In summary, the statement that communication is necessary for leadership carries with it the implication of effective communication. Yet, as the preceding discussion should demonstrate, much is required for effective communication. The leader needs to give attention to and develop skills in each of the elements of communication.

Leadership for an Information Infrastructure Involving Electronic Publishing

The contention that the convergence of libraries and computer centers provides the opportunity for librarians to lead in the development of an information infrastructure, which will include electronic publishing, is not meant to imply that this infrastructure will develop rapidly and immediately from the efforts of individual librarians as they deal with their computer center peers. As the access report notes, the extension of the information infrastructure to electronic publishing is an enormous task that will stretch over years.[16] Rather, this convergence should be seen as an opportunity to develop an understanding of the values of librarians, and an opportunity to begin the movement toward this infrastructure. As librarians deal more and more with computer center personnel, they can begin to convey some of the visions and values of librarianship to these people. In addition, when the chance arises, discussion of practical means for achieving these goals can be initiated.

In one way, it is the opportunity that is most important here. As the LAMA task force report reminds its readers, the statement of a significant goal does little to achieve it. Some practical means need to be available so that actions toward the goal can be initiated. Since the practical means through which librarians can influence those outside the profession to seek goals of significance to librarians are few, each opportunity to do so needs to be recognized and then used to advantage. So, as these units come together, librarians need to recognize the chance to lead and take advantage of it.

Communication: The Language of Leadership

Leadership is much more than communication. The leader must first have vision—must recognize values and goals not readily perceived by others. Next, a leader needs to be able to move others toward some objective; she or he needs to energize, to motivate. Communication is, however, clearly essential for leadership. It is required if one is to communicate a vision or goal, and it is required if one is to motivate. This centrality of communication for leadership, then, requires that the leader's communication be effective. This chapter suggests that this is both difficult yet possible since communication skills can be learned.

The fact that communication skills can be learned is another reason why communication should get the attention of librarians interested in leadership. The abilities to envision and to energize are, more frequently than not, traits of particular kinds of people. They are not skills that can be learned, but rather abilities with which one is born. Thus, those, interested in improving leadership would seem well advised to pay special attention to communication, the aspect of leadership with which one need not to be born.

Leadership for the Public Good

This description of the opportunity for leadership presented by the convergence of libraries and computer centers, and of the importance of communication if librarians are to take advantage of this opportunity, is but one example of leadership for the public good. There are many goals important to society at large that librarians do perceive more clearly than most. Equal access to information, freedom from censorship, and the privacy of one's use of a library are but three of these. Librarians ought to lead toward these goals, and effective communication will be required if they are to do so. An appropriate response, then, to those who urge greater leadership from librarians, and for those who desire to exert more leadership in the world outside the profession, is attention to increasing one's communication skills.

References

1. John W. Gardner, *The Nature of Leadership: Leadership Papers/1* (Washington, D.C.: Independent Sector, 1986), 32–35; Herbert S. White, "Oh, Where Have All the Leaders Gone?" *Library Journal* (October 1, 1987): 68–69; Abraham Zaleznik, "Managers and Leaders: Are They Different?" *Harvard Business Review* (May/June 1977): 67–78.
2. American Library Association, Commission on Freedom and Equal-

ity of Access to Information, *Freedom and Equality of Access to Information* (Chicago: American Library Association, 1986), 1–16.

3. Ibid., 16.
4. David R. Smith, *LAMA Board of Directors, 1986–89*, Document no. 4.2.1 (Chicago: American Library Association, Library Administration and Management Association, 1987), 6.
5. Ibid., 5.
6. Judith Axler Turner, "Columbia U.'s Head Librarian Is Now Managing Academic Computing, Too," *Chronicle of Higher Education* (April 9, 1986): 39–40.
7. Douglas E. Van Houweling, "The Information Technology Environment of Higher Education," in *Campus of the Future: Conference on Information Resources* (Dublin, Ohio: OCLC, 1987), 60–73.
8. Richard M. Dougherty, "Libraries and Computing Centers: A Blueprint for Collaboration," *College & Research Libraries* 48 (1987): 289–96.
9. Ronald B. Adler and George Rodman, *Understanding Human Communication* (New York: Holt, 1985), 11–16.
10. Ibid., 13–14.
11. Ibid., 14.
12. Polley A. McClure, "The Future of Academic Computing: Electronic Library," *BACSpace* (June 1987): 1–6.
13. Ibid., 5.
14. Pat Molholt, "On Converging Paths: The Computing Center and the Library," *Journal of Academic Librarianship* 5 (1985): 284–88.
15. Adler and Rodman, *Human Communication*, 74–77.
16. American Library Association, *Access to Information*, 111.

16

Discourses of Vision and Necessity: The Information Age, the Library, and the Language of Leadership

RICHARD H. MOUL

This chapter will focus on the point of contact between the library and other dimensions of an information society where knowledge has become increasingly fragmented and exteriorized. It will discuss the professional discourse of librarianship, examining its relevance to the current situation and its capacity as a "language of leadership." Those who occupy leadership roles, formal or informal, shape the dialogue within an organization (or profession) in such a way that it mobilizes the community to meet challenges and opportunities imposed by the external environment. Unless members of a community "speak the same language," there is little possibility for effective action.

Douglas MacGregor identified at least four major components of leadership, each of which involves communication in some way or another. These are: the leader's characteristics; the follower's characteristics; the organization's nature; and the external environment's social, economic, political, and cultural facets. These components, in MacGregor's words, mean that "leadership is not a property of the individual, but a complex relationship."[1]

Leadership involves articulating cultural values and establishing the purposes for which a group engages in action. It involves articulating visions and translating them into action. A leader is responsible for the establishment of the boundaries within which activities will be carried out and the criteria by which the group can measure its accomplishments.

Common discourse may be seen as the crucial element in the interface between all of the variables in the leadership relationship. The increasing centrality of information and knowledge, as well as revolutionary changes in the mechanisms for their transmission, requires librarians to understand the relationships between the various aspects of our profession and its external environment. Further, it requires us to reaffirm a forceful statement of our professional role in the cultural, political, and social realms. This reaffirmation is vital for two reasons. First, librarianship is a well-placed profession to influence the positive development of the information society. Second, without a sufficient understanding of our role in supporting a responsible, reasonable, and pluralistic democratic vision, we will lose our distinctiveness as a unique body of information and knowledge workers. We will be losing our voice to systems analysts, computer specialists, MBAs, information entrepreneurs, and other worthy information workers who frequently have narrower views of their responsibilities in society. Such a scenario is worrisome both in terms of our profession's development and for the nature of the world we live in. If libraries are to retain their synergistic (and beneficial) relationship with the realms of knowledge, our leaders will need to continue to foster paradigms that accurately represent current political, economic, social, and cultural situations, as well as appropriate strategic and tactical plans of action.

MacGregor's leadership relationship underscores the "artificial" nature of an organization. Herbert A. Simon has defined an artifact "as a meeting point . . . between an 'inner' environment and the surrounding in which it operates."[2] An organization, then, can be seen as an artifact, or a system, constructed through the interactions of its members as they go about defining an inner environment. Their success is determined by the system's ability to achieve goals established by the organization as it projects these values into the outer world. In systems thought, the success of an "artifact" such as the library is held to be a function of its ability to structure the inner resources at its disposal in order to adapt to changing circumstances. We have at hand the element of a model of the interaction between the library and society.

As Michael K. Buckland has pointed out, libraries are "open systems." This is simply a way of saying that they are affected by, and in turn affect, the world outside their doors.[3] What are the elements of this open system? We could say that the values and practices of librarianship constitute the system's inner realm. Using these resources, we configure our responses to changes in society. The state of knowledge and the role of information in society make up the library's outer environment, which is largely responsible for determining the demands made upon libraries by users. The leadership relationship in our profession is a discourse about the design and implementation of an artifact that accommodates the library's operation to the necessities imposed by developments in society.

I will make two general observations before examining the point of contact between the inner realm of librarianship and the discourses of societal knowledge. First, I offer a caveat concerning my use of the language of systems theory. Systems thought tends to look at an interface in terms of how well the internal nature of the artifact is able to adapt, or conform, to dictates imposed by the external world. In other words, systems thinkers look primarily at the artifact in terms of its performance.[4] Obviously, the library's "performance" is a key component of what we want to explore when we concern ourselves with librarianship. Indeed, many argue cogently that a lack of emphasis on performance is one of the weaknesses of our professional discourse. We have a difficult time establishing criteria for judging how well our services contribute to the needs generated out in the external world.[5] That said, it should be noted that there is a snare that the systems approach may trap us in. Performance is an outlook that imposes some hidden assumptions on the analyst. If we are not careful, the performative dimension of the systems approach will lead us to accept a particular set of values from the external world without examining the internal values of our profession in order to validate these criteria as our primary goals.[6] As professionals, we have a responsibility to society to project our beliefs about the nature of knowledge, information, and communication in community life into discussions of questions concerning these elements outside our doors. Such discussions require some hard thought about our inner and outer environments.[7] José Ortega y Gasset argues that the duty of the "librarian has varied in direct proportion to the significance of the book as a social necessity."[8] Ortega y Gasset is speaking of a mission that is created through the discourse of a community assessing its historical situation. While the question of performance at the level of the task environment is obviously of critical importance to the effectiveness of library service, it is not the appropriate criteria to use in defining the mission of the library. Such an approach enframes the concept of the library's mission in a performative economic paradigm that undercuts the library's responsibilities in political and cultural contexts. The discourse of librarianship must begin with an account of the fullest relationship between the institution and society.

My second preliminary observation involves answering the question, In what sense am I using the term *discourse*? A dictionary will tell us that we are dealing with a "verbal interchange of ideas; especially conversation." Right at the outset we are involved with communication. Further, discourse is "connected speech or writing." Thus, the concept incorporates the notion of a formal, interactive, communicative process. Discourse can be seen as conversation, or discussion, that is formulated according to some sort of standards or rules. These rules involve the form and context of messages, or "speech acts," introduced into the conversation, as well as the criteria used for examining and judging these new entries into the discussion, and the accreditation of participants.

Discourse has become an axial, or organizing, principle in the work of a number of social observers. Theorists such as Michael Foucault, François Lyotard, and Jurgen Habermas—to name a few—have focused on it as a central feature in the creation of community life. A major concern of these writers is the relationship between knowledge and power in society. Consequently, they focus on the role of discourses in providing access to power and in legitimating its role within a group. As Lyotard points out, "the social bond is linguistic."[9] These observers have undertaken detailed analyses of the role of language, communication, information, and knowledge in community life. Discourse is both the object and the method of their efforts.

John E. Toews, an intellectual historian, has posited two variants of a theory of discourse.[10] One centers around the use of language in establishing the structural relationship between theory, practice, and judgment to constitute the relatively restrictive patterns of communication in disciplines. This approach, based largely on the work of Foucault, develops a theory of "the discourse of language" generated in their study of disciplines. Foucault develops a theory of social rules whereby "the production of discourse is at once controlled, selected, organized, and redistributed according to a certain number of procedures whose role is to avert its powers and dangers, to cope with chance events, and to evade its ponderous, awesome materiality."[11] From Foucault's point of view, the key object in the analysis is the power structure that restricts discourse in various settings. Paradigms, according to Thomas S. Kuhn, are sets of assumptions and beliefs.[12] They are uncontested as long as they adequately explain the results of research. They lose their power to hold practitioners together when they fail to account for anomalies that an accepted theory cannot explain. The process through which paradigms are created and discarded is discursive.

The conception of discourse as the foundation of public life has been a major theme in the work of Jurgen Habermas, who has presented a detailed theory for analyzing the speech acts underlying discourse, as well as an analysis of the breakdown of the discourses underpinning the institutions of the modern age. For Habermas, free discourse is an essential component of an ideal society: the key task facing us is the establishment of structures for communication that provide all participants in social discourse with a "symmetrical distribution of chances to select and employ speech acts. Thus, the conditions for ideal discourse are connected to conditions for an ideal form of life." [13]

Several themes run through the ideas discussed here. First, all are built upon the notion of the fundamental importance of "speech acts," or the individual's contribution to the creation of a discourse through which a community is constituted—be the community a group of researchers, a profession, an organization, or a public institution. Second, all are concerned with the rules by which these actions are authorized and by which they are judged. Finally, they all concern the relationship between speech, or communication, and power. The ability to control or divert discourse confers power.

These notions can be used to focus our attention on some of the key aspects of the leadership relation in librarianship. Peering inward, the discourses that transpire in our professional circles and libraries will be seen to have much to do with the success in meeting obligations. These conversations prepare the ground for action by building our corporate culture. Looking outward, we will find that the necessities facing the library in an information society are closely related to the conservation of free discourse.

It is my belief, that I have clearly established the position from which I wish to examine the leadership relation in librarianship. We are standing at the juncture of our profession and its outer world: our society at large. We know that leadership involves articulating a meaning for our profession that goes deeper than an analysis of our performance at the level of the task environment; it requires us to discuss the social necessities that give rise to our profession. Finally, we are cognizant that in order to lead we must either reconstruct or establish a discourse of librarianship that will inform our performance at the task-environment level with the knowledge of our importance to society. The next step, then, is an examination of the outer world, which brings us to a discussion of information and knowledge in our society.

The External Dimension

It is now commonplace to say that we live in the information age. About half of our work force is engaged in information work of one sort of another. During the 1970s, the information sector of the major western economies surpassed the agricultural, industrial, and service sectors in each of these economies. In macroeconomic analysis, the bottom line is usually measured in terms of gross national product (GNP). Mark U. Porat's well-known calculations have shown that by 1967, close to half of the U.S. GNP was generated through some sort of information-related activity.[14] Additionally, the phenomenal growth in the volume of information during the postwar era—one estimate is that the rate of "increase has been so exponential that we have been able to generate more *printed* [emphasis added] information in the past ten years than in mankind's complete history"—gives us an indication of its increasing importance.[15] Yet what do these data really mean? After all, as Norman D. Stevens recently pointed out, "information has long played, in one fashion or another, a key role in society." The problem, Stevens says, is that "we have not dealt adequately with the concept of information as a historical force."[16] In a sense, Stevens points out the significance of the changes taking place today. We have now begun to recognize the centrality of information and knowledge. What signals the emergence of an information age is the development of discourses built around "information." Indeed, information has become a key metaphor in our approach to the world. Beyond their empirical significance (in itself breathtaking), the data discussed here are evidence of this transition in our conversations.

Several developments provide the images of our discussions in the information age. The first of these is structural. The connection of telecommunications systems to computers has blurred the "distinction between processing and communications." Data, technology, and organizational structures have been linked to create a revolutionary information-infrastructure. Herbert A. Simon considers this linkage to have implications on par with the development of writing and printing. He calls this the "third information revolution."[17] This information infrastructure is constructed around what J. David Bolter has termed the "defining technology" of the information age—the computer. Much as the clock served as the metaphor for the mechanistic cosmology of Descartes and Copernicus, the computer is changing our outlook on the world: "The computer is giving us a new definition of man, as an 'information processor,' and of nature as 'information to be processed.' "[18] Bolter sees evidence of this change in the languages of various social science disciplines: the cognitive psychologist "begins to study the mind's 'algorithm' for searching long-term memory"; the economist uses input-output diagrams; the sociologist studies "quantitative history"; and the "humanist . . . prepares a 'key-word-in-context' concordance."

Daniel Bell believes that a distinctive problem of the information age is the management of "organized complexity." A characteristic of the postindustrial milieu is the need to manage large systems with many variables. Many techniques for treating these questions have emerged since World War II. Bell calls methods like those mentioned above "intellectual technologies." These "technologies," rooted primarily in probability theory, typically substitute "algorithms for intuitive judgments." Their goals involve " 'ordering' the mass society." [19]

The information theory unveiled with the publication of Claude Shannon's two 1948 papers dealing with the transmission of messages has emerged as an essential feature of the discourse on the information society. [20] A consequence of this development is the recognition of the status of information as a critical commodity. While having special properties, information becomes subject to market and political forces more directly than ever before. As Blaise Cronin has observed, "Information may be intangible, but the market now recognizes that information can, in some respects, be treated like any other commodity." [21] Thus far, we have focused on computers and information as key components of the discourse affecting the library from the outside. As the library has traditionally concerned itself with the stock of public knowledge, a fair question to ask here is, What is the status of knowledge in the information society? Bell argues that one of the central features of the new social order is the centrality of theoretical knowledge:

> The advances in a field become increasingly dependent upon the primacy of theoretical work which codifies what is known and points the way to empirical confirmation. In effect, theoretical knowledge becomes the strategic resource, the axial principle of a society, and the university, research organizations, and intellectual institutions, where theoretical knowledge is codified and enriched, become the axial structures of the emergent society. [22]

For Bell, theoretical knowledge "consists of new judgments." It is "an organized set of statements . . . presenting a reasoned judgment or an experimental result." These are "transmitted . . . in some systematic form." [23] A key point here is the emphasis on communication and judgment. These are, as was pointed out earlier, the components of a discourse.

When we untie knowledge from its status as a "structure or an edifice" [24] and focus on the communicative aspects that go into producing, validating, and judging it, at least three interrelated issues emerge. The first of these involves legitimation: How do we judge statements made within a discourse? The second concerns the fragmentation of knowledge: How do the many diverse conversations interrelate? Finally, there is the pivotal question of how knowledge relates to power: Since we have seen that information has been transformed into a commodity, it is worthwhile to ask, Is there a corollary involving knowledge?

These questions should be of concern to librarians interested in leading their profession in the information age. One last point: these issues are unfolding in a time when the discourse concerning the nature of the public welfare in American society is also in turmoil. The terms defining our community life are undergoing intense scrutiny from many sides. As members of a profession tied overwhelmingly to public organization, librarians need to discuss these questions, and library leaders will have to help shape the discourse. At issue here is the nature of discourse in our society, as well as the question of access to discussions. The first is a matter of legitimacy; the second is a matter of power. The status of information and knowledge are axial components of these discussions.

Legitimacy involves judging and validating. It is a question of communication. According to Habermas, discourse involves the capacity to create a consensual "normative reality" where participants use agreed-upon criteria to judge the understandability, truth, sincerity, and appropriateness of statements entered into a discussion. These "validity claims," as he calls them, are implied in most of the discourses in which we engage. However, in discussions where paradigms are contested, where "the background consensus is fundamentally called into question," disputed claims can only be assessed "by entering into a discourse whose sole purpose is to judge the truth of the problematic opinion, or the correctness of a problematic norm."[25]

That there is a crisis of legitimacy—a wide-scale rejection of one another's terms for discourse—in the information society is widely noted. Daniel Bell has developed this issue as a theory of "disjunction" between the social structure and cultural realms of postindustrial society. For Bell, society contains three realms, each operating under the terms of its own discourses: The *social structure* (which includes the economy, technology, and the occupational system) is dominated by a discourse of economizing; the *culture* (the realm of expressive symbolism and meanings) is grounded in a discussion of self-fulfillment; and the *polity* (which regulates the distribution of power and the mediation of individual and group claims) is dominated by a discourse of participation.[26]

Many social theorists conceive of these features as components of a unitary system where regulation and control ultimately seek to generate harmony. Bell agrees that in the past these realms were held together by common values and character structure. This is no longer the case. Each realm has developed its own language and poses questions and challenges for the others. They tend to propel discussion along increasingly antagonistic lines. Actors belonging primarily to one discourse or another frequently talk past each other. Bell pointed this out in a seminal passage written in 1965:

The high degree of specialization—both in the fields of knowledge as well as in the structures of organizations—inevitably creates an almost unbearable strain between "the culture" and the social structure. In fact, it becomes quite difficult to speak even of "the" culture, for not only do specializations create "subcultures" or private worlds—in the anthropological sense—but these in turn create private languages and private signs and symbols which often . . . infiltrate the "public" world of culture.

Today, the culture can hardly, if at all, reflect the society in which people live. The system of social relations is so complex and differentiated, and experiences so specialized, complicated or incomprehensible, that it is difficult to find common symbols of meaning to relate one experience to another.[27]

François Lyotard, a French philosopher, has written an interesting essay concerning communicative problems. Starting from the proposition that science, culture, and politics all have their foundation in discourse, he analyzes how these discourses interact with each other, how the dynamics of these interactions affect the status of knowledge, and the relationship between these questions and power.

In addition to fragmenting culture, theoretical (or scientific) knowledge actually undercuts "customary" knowledge. Lyotard explains how this happens in terms of legitimation. While science is marketed as a quest to build a coherent body of knowledge, it is actually a discourse legitimated by "paralogy," or the search of fallacy. Science expands when a traditional paradigm no longer explains questions raised in normal research. After debate, a new paradigm may emerge. Lyotard argues that this constant probing of legitimacy is the cornerstone of science. Consequently, it is involved in a discourse that will continually fragment as new games emerge.[28] On the other hand, customary knowledge is built on discourses designed to establish consensual norms or traditions. These discussions rarely withstand scientific probing of their legitimacy.

Knowledge in the information society has been "exteriorized" and turned into a tool for use by the agencies of the social structure and the state. This knowledge, generated as it has been through the discourses of intellectual technology, is likely to reflect its source.[29] Since "knowledge is power" in a very literal sense, access to it and to the information constituting it are key political issues. The structure of discourse in the realms of science, politics, and ethics contains a "strict interlinkage." They involve the question of legitimation—of judgment. Lyotard believes

knowledge and power are simply two sides of the same question; who decides what knowledge is and who decides what needs to be decided. In the computer age, the question of knowledge is now more than ever a question of government.[30]

Political power has been seen by many social theorists as the ability of a social system to "get things done in the interest of collective goals."[31] The first aspect of this definition, the ability to "get things done," expresses an instrumental, or performative, aspect of power. Performance, the effectiveness or efficiency of the means used in getting something done, is commonly the major criterion for assessing power. Discussions often focus on what might more accurately be called force, strength, or violence. This emphasis leads to discussions of the means available for acting.

Hannah Arendt believes that power in political discussion should be distinguished from the ability to get things done (force). Further, it is grounded in legitimacy. In turn, this is based on free and open discourse among those participating in the public realm.[32] The relevance of Arendt's concept of constitutive power for the information society lies in its ability to focus attention on both the access citizens have to information and their ability to judge the meanings supplied by the agencies involved in the generation of discourse. The degree of access and the ability to use information and knowledge in public discourse become fundamental components of political power.

If we have failed to recognize the role information (and by implication knowledge) has played in the unfolding of societies, a discourse concerning the relationships between these variables is long overdue. The stakes here are much higher than many of us realize. Just as information has become a key metaphor for many current explanations of nature, and the tools used in this pursuit have become defining technologies for many thinkers, knowledge has come to the forefront as the pivotal component of both instrumental and constitutive power. Indeed, this can be stated plainly: The axial struggle of the age will be over which discourse of power will inform our view of knowledge. The information age is one where learning will circulate "along the same lines as money." As knowledge circulates, the control and access channels of communication and centers of codification become pivotal.[33]

Three dangers characteristic to the information society cohere around this transformation of information into a *recognized* commodity and of knowledge into capital. Two are relatively straightforward and have been much discussed in the library literature. First, private-sector charges for information services may price many out of the marketplace, and hence out of the discussion. Second, there is no guarantee that concerns based on the value of a commodity will not be indifferent to data that is not clearly marketable. Some materials may drop out of society's pool of accessible knowledge.[34]

An issue that is less obvious involves managing the wealth of information. A problem characterizing the information society stems from the fact that humans are simply incapable of processing huge volumes of data coming from a multitude of sources quickly enough to make many decisions effectively. The capacity to turn information into knowledge expeditiously—forming the basis for decisions—becomes a tremendous competitive advantage. Overload, or "meaning lag," creates strategic positions along the channels of communications for gatekeepers. Individuals must rely on these programmers in their attempt to become informed. As Bruce Gates points out, most of us are captive of "specialized roles, beliefs, and ways of thinking as supplied by those who control (or package) information."[35]

Gates argues that belief, rather than knowledge, "is the antecedent to practical instrumental action." In other words, while we use theoretical knowledge as a resource in decision making, narratively based customary knowledge is what prompts us to act. Since beliefs are built on discourse, the danger is that

> access to information for the purpose of increasing political awareness and for informing public opinion, will be largely controlled by those with a stake in what our personal organizing principles are.[36]

What Gates is driving at is that discourse in the information society will be based not only on the data available to individuals, but also on the ways in which information is framed by those in a position to disseminate it. Moreover, the control over information allows the controller a tremendous advantage in setting agendas. Gates continues:

> What these organizing principles are or will become is important because they will determine the ground rules underlying the production of knowledge—or more correctly belief-based "communities."[37]

Access to the "intellectual commons" is not the only concern in the maintenance of free discourse. The ability to obtain information must be coupled with an ability to name the gatekeepers and identify their agendas.

As the application of economizing principles to information increasingly becomes the norm, "public-sector information utilities" such as libraries "may find themselves pushed to the periphery."[38] What librarians are confronting is an outgrowth of the rise of the axiality of information and knowledge, which threatens to consign them to a marginal role in the information society.

The marginalizing of public information sources is vigorously pursued at the policy level in the United States today. During the past few years, an assault on the right to access information has been conducted primarily under the guise of a campaign for administrative efficiency. There has been a largely successful attempt to establish a de facto national information policy where information is not a free good but a resource of substantial economic value and should be treated as such. Also, any information to be disseminated to the public must "pass the supreme test of cost-benefit analysis." The factors weighed in such determinations were assigned by people within the Reagan administration who were already party to the information (and who, it goes without saying, have particular interests) that is being judged. Through executive order, the dismantling of access to information concerning public matters is well advanced. The recent request for proposals for contracting out the National Technical Information Service is but one example of this trend.[39]

I have indicated the roles that access to information and knowledge, as well as the ability to judge the messages used to convey them, play in maintaining free discourse. Further, I have discussed the role of this discourse in maintaining democratic governance. Presently, the trend in the public realm is to emphasize a concept of "self-sufficiency" grounded in civil liberty, but mostly in economic rationality, as compared with a concept of "mutual dependence" in the discourse concerning public welfare. Tension between these opposite views has created a duality that has guided discourse in the American political tradition since the nation's beginnings.[40]

Currently, this discourse implies that knowledge is to be governed primarily by a discourse of "economizing" rather than "political participation." The organizing principles of this discourse—or at least the information, knowledge, and filtering systems required to develop them—are slipping from the grasp of an informed citizenry. Thomas Jefferson identified the stakes involved in 1816 with the observation that "if a nation expects to be ignorant and free, in a state of civilization, it expects what never was and never will be."[41] How does librarianship fit into the information society? How will the "substance and organization" of the library adapt to meet the challenges posed by its external environment? How will librarians respond to the "the social necessity which the profession serves?" In order to discuss these questions, we need to turn our focus inward and examine the discourses that inform our responses to the world outside our doors.

The Internal Dimension

At the outset, I identified the communicative nature of leadership and emphasized MacGregor's belief that leadership is fundamentally a relationship. At its best, this relationship involves the constitutive power that

Arendt spoke of. Good leaders harness this power, turning it into effective planning and action. In a recent book on leadership, John P. Kotter reviewed studies of effective managers at various echelons in public and private organizations. He concluded:

> The effective leadership of a project team located ten layers below the CEO in a larger corporation and the overall effective leadership of the overall corporation by the CEO both seem to share some fundamentals in common: a good vision and strategy backed up by sufficient teamwork and motivation.[42]

He distills this into two factors found in effective leadership of complex organizations: "Creating an agenda for change, and building a strong implementation network."

The notions of discourse summarized earlier are pertinent to the cultivation of both of these factors. Ultimately, it is through the constitutive power of communicative acts that organizations and institutions establish their agendas and build their networks.

In discussing the inner realm of librarianship, we must first consider the levels at which our discourses take place and how they interact. Peering inward, an observer might find discussions operating along three major pathways. At the level nearest the interface with the outside world, one would encounter a metadiscourse concerning the role of libraries in society. Discussions would highlight fundamental missions and services that librarians undertake. These would include discussion of archival responsibilities, the provision of access to information, and the library's educational missions. The discussion of these roles would follow a multiplicity of patterns as participants from various backgrounds engaged with each other. Within the discussion generated from all of these locales, there is embedded a key question, What is the nature of libraries? Regarding "the library," can we legitimately speak of a unified concept, employing some kind of notion of a library network of Alexandrian scope? Are we dealing with an institution or merely with units inside of other social agencies? Treatment of these questions is clouded because the metadiscourse of the profession rests on a shaky substrata of shifting organizational and disciplinary discussions.

Due to the various types of libraries and aspects of librarianship, our observer's picture is muddied further by competing claims arising from within different units of individual organizations. Even within a single library, there are the competing languages of the cataloger, reference librarian, provider of bibliographic instruction, administrator, and so on. To use Bell's terminology, at least two disjunctions can be adduced to account for these gulfs. One is a difference between the languages of public

and technical services; the other is a disjunction between the discourses
of administration and operative staff. In a report commissioned by the
Academic Research Libraries Personnel Study Group of ACRL, Allen B.
Veaner (lamenting the "atomization endemic to the profession") observed:

> We debate the profession's inability to speak with one voice, yet the re-
> sponsible forces may be the same ones that divide the entire academic
> establishment into so many parts. Institutional structures, such as hi-
> erarchy and departmentation in the larger research libraries, assist the
> process to the point where isolationism can develop to ridiculous de-
> grees.[43]

He wonders whether this fragmentation "merely reflects the general
academic fragmentation that has characterized research since the 19th
Century." One would certainly hope not—librarianship by paralogy, to
appropriate from Lyotard, clearly will not do.

Yet we seem to have a difficult time of it when we try to communicate
with one another about matters of central importance to the profession.
It is not tremendously reassuring to read, for example, that in 1987

> getting librarians and administrators to view their respective roles realis-
> tically and work together constructively in a collegial, congenial, trusting
> partnership would seem to be the top priority.[44]

As if this were a major revelation. Or, that knowing

> the social, economic and political context in which the library operates
> is "not as high a priority as knowledge of one's discipline." For "these
> contexts are not as important as leadership in being effective."[45]

or, again, that

> the bewildered groping which characterizes so much of our activity is
> largely the result of lack of definite conception of our purposes.[46]

We realize that these last words, written in 1934, resonate so well
today. Why should we be surprised when our competitors in the information society, the purveyors of "instant information" in Hollywood and
Madison Avenue, mock us in soda commercials and comic book–level
movies about ghosts?

Perhaps I have stuffed my strawperson a bit too full, or possibly even
misunderstood the context of these particular speech acts. But it remains
that, on the whole, we have not done a really good job legitimating our
profession or the institution we serve. One measure of this is the disrespect
the external world shows the M.L.S. degree in assessing our capabilities.

An even crueler twist is an unwarranted statement by a library director that "so many members of our profession do not have a strong intellectual commitment to librarianship."[47]

Professional leadership is about creating the discourse by which we will constitute an "agenda for change" and build the networks we require to implement it. Library leaders must recognize this necessity. Fortunately many do. In *Library Leadership: Visualizing the Future* some of our professional leaders grapple with what leadership means within their particular disciplinary matrices.[48] It is instructive to hear what some of them have to say. Carolyn Dusenbury defines leadership as the exercise of influence. She says, "The exercise of influence is that of making things happen, of mobilizing and organizing toward the accomplishment of goals." For her, leadership in reference is the development of a theory of reference service. Her premise is "that a theoretical foundation that is widely practiced and understood can help reference librarians solve common problems and also help them to anticipate the issues they will face in the next 20 years." This discourse will catalyze bibliographic instruction, computer-assisted reference service, the evaluation of reference services, and rights to information access.[49]

Michael Gorman develops the distinction between leadership and administration. This involves vision: "The essential difference between management/administration on one hand and leadership on the other, is that the former is concerned with *what is* and the latter is concerned with *what will be*." Leaders in technical services must be willing to "adapt the organization of technical services, rationalize, accept the implications of automation, and engage in useful and realistic cooperation."[50]

For Edward E. Shaw, leadership requires the "courage to fail." In order to minimize the failure of our leaders, he focuses on the need to understand the relationship between the university and the library, the impact of technology on the library, and the relationships between strategic planning, governance, and leadership.[51]

These essays provide us with many of the elements we need to develop a forceful discourse of librarianship. They also emphasize the librarian's role as a manger. This emphasis is especially crucial, if, as many observers have argued, the professional librarian is "shifting from production to management." If this is true, our professional discourse must support the necessary changes in outlook. The challenge for leaders will be to develop a discourse that will nurture talented, creative administrators (leaders) who recognize that obligations to long-term employees include creating a challenging and satisfying work environment where daily problems are confronted directly. In other words, within our departments, the language of leadership involves the promotion of an institutional culture that will sustain "implementation networks." The ability to do so involves the ability to transmit a cogent vision of what it is all about: Motivation.

A problem facing many libraries, however, is the instability of cultural traditions. After discussing the importance of philosophy in eloquent terms, David W. Lewis observes:

> Organizational philosophies generally begin at the top, and as we have seen, academic library directors may not stay in one place long enough to leave their mark. In addition, advancement in academic librarianship often requires movement between institutions. Without stability, the cultural traditions of the organization are lost.[52]

Ironically, knowledge-conserving organizations have difficulty maintaining their institutional memory.

Clearly, in J. Periam Danton's 1934 "Pleas for a Philosophy of Librarianship" there is a relevant topic of conversation for us today. The language of leadership requires the articulation of vision. This discourse must proceed from an accounting of "all the relevant organizational and environmental forces."[53] It must involve a discussion of our "facticity," or role in the information society. Most of the foregoing has concerned academic libraries, but it applies across the board in the library world.

Conclusion

The primary role of the library is the preservation of knowledge. In fulfilling this mission, the library exercises an institutional role in society. Social institutions such as the family, the polity, the social structure, and the culture are the locations of the discourses through which we are able to build communities. The organizations that transform our institutions into social reality are generally seen as secondary institutions or social agencies. Thus, major concepts such as the family, religion, or law define the outlines of society, while agencies such as courts and churches are shaped by the outlines. (The primary actors in the discourse of the institutions may well be the workers in the agencies.) As we have seen, these institutions are pulling away from each other, and many of the agencies supporting them have a difficult time legitimating themselves. We are not the only ones with problems characterized by the information age.

The library, ultimately, is responsible for the preservation of knowledge. No other body has accepted this mission. It therefore takes on the cast of an institution, even though most libraries are embedded in other organizations.

The librarian is also an agent charged with empowering people by providing access to knowledge. As against those in the "instant information" business, the librarian is, or ought to be, a gatekeeper who uses the position to help individuals "decide what is important" for themselves. Lester Asheim points out the uniqueness of the librarian in this regard:

> More than any other gatekeeper in the field of formal communication, the librarian is devoted to the tradition of individual service and individual response . . . the individual exchange remains the keystone of the library's service.[54]

Joan M. Bechtel is surely on the right track when she asks in the title of an article in *College & Research Libraries*, "Conversation, a New Paradigm for Librarianship?" She answers that "libraries bear the critical burden of preserving, facilitating, and participating in" the discourse of the information society.[55] Leadership in the profession means helping to shape the conversation.

The conversation must involve the establishment of an agenda that deals with the realities of the information age and helps us to develop means for responding to challenges to individual access and participation in the intellectual commons of our society. There are a lot of permutations and levels for our talks. Debates concerning "fee versus free" or the "paperless society," for example, are useful to us if we use them to build up the quality of our professional discourse. Similarly, discussions between different branches of the profession should always take into account our ultimate purposes as a way of bridging gaps. What we do at the task-environment level is not the end, but the means. One thing we should always be mindful of: What Jefferson pointed out in the agricultural age is no less true in the information age—a society cannot be ignorant *and* free.

References

1. Douglas MacGregor, *Leadership and Motivation* (Cambridge, Mass.: MIT Press, 1966), 73–74.
2. Herbert A. Simon, *The Science of the Artificial*, 2d ed. (Cambridge, Mass.: MIT Press, 1981), 8–10.
3. Michael K. Buckland, *Library Services in Theory and Context* (New York: Pergamon, 1983), 29–33.
4. Ida R. Hoos, *Systems Analysis in Public Policy: A Critique* (Berkeley: University of California Press, 1972), 248–49.
5. G. Travis White, "Quantitative Measures of Library Effectiveness," *Journal of Academic Librarianship* 3 (July 1977): 128.

6. Martin Heidegger, *The Question concerning Technology and Other Essays* (New York: Harper & Row, 1977), 3–55.

7. Lester Asheim, "Librarians as Professionals," *Library Trends* 27 (Winter 1979): 225–57.

8. José Ortega y Gasset, *The Mission of the Librarian*, trans. James Lewis and Ray Carpenter, (Boston: G. K. Hall, 1961), 7.

9. François Lyotard, *The Post-Modern Condition: A Report on Knowledge* (Minneapolis: University of Minnesota Press, 1984), 40.

10. John E. Towes, "Intellectual History after the Linguistic Turn: The Autonomy of Meaning and the Irreducibility of Experience," *American Historical Review* 92 (October 1987): 897–907.

11. Michael Foucault, *The Archeology of Knowledge and the Discourse on Language* (New York: Pantheon, 1972), 216.

12. Thomas S. Kuhn, *The Structure of Scientific Revolutions*, 2d ed., enlarged (Chicago: University of Chicago Press, 1970).

13. Thomas McCarthy, "Introduction," in Jurgen Habermas, *Legitimation Crisis* (Boston: Beacon, 1975), xvii.

14. Tjerk Huppes, *The Western Edge: Work and Management in the Information Age* (Dordrecht, The Netherlands: Kluwer, 1987), 9–17.

15. Henry M. Kibirige, *The Information Dilemma: A Critical Analysis of Information Pricing and the Fees Controversy* (Westport, Conn.: Greenwood, 1983), 6.

16. Norman D. Stevens, "The History of Information," in *Advances in Librarianship*, vol. 4 (Orlando: Academic Press, 1986), 1.

17. Herbert A. Simon, "What Computers Mean for Man and Society," *Science* 195 (March 18, 1977): 1186.

18. J. David Bolter, *Turning's Man: Western Culture in the Computer Age* (Chapel Hill: University of North Carolina Press, 1984), 13.

19. Daniel Bell, *The Coming of Post-Industrial Society: A Venture in Social Forecasting* (New York: Basic, 1973), 30.

20. Jeremy Campbell, *Grammatical Man: Information, Entropy, Language and Life* (New York: Simon & Schuster, 1982), 46.

21. Blaise Cronin, "The Information Society," *ASLIB Proceedings* 34 (April 1985): 127.

22. Daniel Bell, "The Social Framework of the Information Society," in *The Computer Age: A Twenty Year View*, eds. Michael Dertouzos and Joel Moses (Cambridge, Mass.: MIT Press, 1979), 168.

23. Bell, *Post-Industrial Society*, 26.

24. Don R. Swanson, "Libraries and the Growth of Knowledge," in *The Role of Libraries in the Growth of Knowledge*, ed. Don R. Swanson (Chicago: University of Chicago Press, 1980), 114–15.

25. Jurgen Habermas, "What Is Universal Pragmatics," in *Communica-*

tion and the Evolution of Society, ed. Jurgen Habermas (Boston: Beacon, 1979), 26–29; McCarthy, "Introduction," xviii–xix.

26. Bell, *Post-Industrial Society*, 114.
27. Daniel Bell, "The Disjunction of Culture and Social Structure: Some Notes on the Meaning of Social Reality," in *Science and Culture: A Study of Disjunctive and Cohesive Forces*, ed. Gerald Holton (Boston: Beacon, 1965), 244.
28. Lyotard, *Post-Modern Condition*, 4–9.
29. Ibid., 40.
30. Ibid., 41.
31. Jurgen Habermas, "Hannah Arendt on the Concept of Power," in *Philosophical-Political Profile*, trans. Thomas McCarthy (Cambridge, Mass.: MIT Press, 1983), 172.
32. Hannah Arendt, *The Human Condition* (Chicago: University of Chicago Press, 1958), 200.
33. Lyotard, *Post-Modern Condition*, 6.
34. Gordon B. Neavill, "Electronic Publishing, Libraries and the Survival of Information," *Library Resources and Technical Services* 28 (January/March 1984): 81–87.
35. Bruce Gates, "Knowledge, Networks and Neighborhoods: Will Microcomputers Make Us Better Citizens?" *Public Administration Review* 44 (March 1984): 167.
36. Ibid.
37. Ibid.
38. Cronin, "Information Society," 128–29.
39. Walter Karp, "Library under Siege: The Reagan Administration's Taste for Autocracy," *Harpers* 271 (November 1985): 53–67.
40. High Heclo, "General Welfare and Two American Political Traditions," *Political Science Quarterly* 101 (1986): 179–96.
41. Thomas Jefferson, "Letter to Colonel Yancey," quoted in *Thomas Jefferson on Democracy*, ed. Saul K. Padover, (New York: Mentor, 1939), 89.
42. John P. Kotter, *The Leadership Factor* (New York: Macmillan, 1988), 19–21.
43. Allen B. Veaner, "1985 to 1995: The Next Decade in Academic Librarianship, Part I," *College & Research Libraries* 46 (May 1985): 215.
44. Brian Alley, "What Professional Librarians Expect from Administrators: An Administrator's Response," *College & Research Libraries* 48 (September 1987): 420.
45. Irene B. Hoadley, "Reactions to 'Defining the Academic Librarian,'" *College & Research Libraries* 46 (November 1985): 469.

46. J. Periam Danton, "Plea for a Philosophy of Librarianship," *Library Quarterly* 4 (October 1934): 527–51.
47. Allen B. Veaner, "1985 to 1995: The Next Decade in Academic Librarianship, Part II," *College & Research Libraries* 46 (July 1985): 302–3.
48. Donald E. Riggs, ed., *Library Leadership: Visualizing the Future* (Phoenix: Oryx Press, 1982).
49. Carolyn Dusenbury, "Reference Service: Software in the Hardware Age," in *Library Leadership: Visualizing the Future*, ed. Donald E. Riggs (Phoenix: Oryx Press, 1982), 73–83.
50. Michael Gorman, "A Good Heart and an Organized Mind: Leadership in Technical Services," in *Library Leadership: Visualizing the Future*, ed. Donald E. Riggs (Phoenix: Oryx Press, 1982), 73–83.
51. Edward E. Shaw, "The Courage to Fail," in *Library Leadership: Visualizing the Future*, ed. Donald E. Riggs (Phoenix: Oryx Press, 1982), 53–65.
52. David W. Lewis, "An Organizational Paradigm for Effective Academic Libraries," *College & Research Libraries* 47 (July 1986): 351.
53. Kotter, *Leadership Factor*, 20.
54. Lester Asheim, "Ortega Revised," *Library Quarterly* 52 (July 1982): 221.
55. Joan M. Bechtel, "Conversation, a New Paradigm for Librarianship?" *College & Research Libraries* 47 (May 1986): 222.

Contributors

Rosemary H. Arneson is currently the director of Everett Library at Queens College, Charlotte, N.C. She received her master's in librarianship in 1982 from Emory University in Atlanta. She has been an active member of ALA and LAMA for several years and has served on the LAMA Membership Committee and the ALA Awards Committee, in addition to several committee appointments for JMRT.

John M. Budd is presently an associate professor with the School of Library and Information Science of Louisiana State University. His doctorate is from the University of North Carolina at Chapel Hill. He has published articles in a number of journals, including *Library Administration & Management*, *College & Research Libraries*, *RQ*, *Journal of Academic Librarianship*, *Library Journal*, *Collection Management*, and others. He has also written a book entitled *The Library and Its Users; The Process of Communication* to be published in 1992.

June D. Chressanthis is an assistant professor and serials cataloger at the Mitchell Memorial Library, Mississippi State University. She received her

AMLS from the University of Michigan in 1983. Her research interests concern organizational communication, the role of leadership in libraries, the organizing and implementing of reclassification projects, and statistical analyses of various forms of price discrimination practiced in the pricing of academic journals. She has presented poster sessions at the ALA Annual Conference as well as state conferences.

E. Anne Edwards is the associate dean for access services at the University of Alabama Libraries in Tuscaloosa. She holds an MLS from the University of Western Ontario, and an MA in Italian studies from Aberdeen University, Scotland. Edwards is an active member of LAMA and ACRL, the current chair of the Alabama chapter of ACRL, and is very interested in management and leadership in the profession.

Barbara B. Fischler has been director of Libraries, Indiana University–Purdue University at Indianapolis since 1981. She has worked in the field of academic librarianship for 26 years. Recently, she was elected vice chair/chair-elect of the LAMA Fund-Raising and Financial Development Section. She is on the board of directors for the Midwest Federation of Library Associations and active in the Indiana Library Association.

Charles D. Hanson is currently director of public libraries, Grosse Pointe, Michigan. He earned an MLS from the University of Wisconsin–Milwaukee and a PhD in English from Bowling Green State University. He has served on various PLA committees as well as LAMA and ACRL committees; his publications have appeared in *College & Research Libraries News* and other journals.

Peggy Johnson is currently assistant director of the St. Paul Campus Libraries, University of Minnesota. She received a BS from St. Olaf College, an MS from the University of Chicago Graduate Library School, and an MBA from Metropolitan State University. Her publications include *Automation and Organizational Change in Libraries* (G. K. Hall, 1991), *Materials Budgets in ARL Libraries*, *SPEC Kit 166* (Association of Research Libraries, 1990), articles on collection development and management and new technologies in libraries, and a regular column in *Technicalities.*

Kelly Janousek is a senior assistant librarian at California State University, Long Beach. Her specialties are business and legal reference and collection development and instruction. She is active in the American Library Association RASD Business Reference Services Section and the Library

Instruction Round Table. Janousek received her MLS from the University of Pittsburgh.

H. Rebecca Kroll earned her MLS and MBA degrees while working in the SUNY Buffalo Libraries. She is now reference librarian at the Lorain County Community College Library in Elyria, Ohio. Her research interests include library automation and application of the theories of organizational behavior in a library setting. She has published articles on staff evaluation in libraries, the direct and indirect effects of automation on the functions of the library, and how to achieve an optimum mix of computerized and other reference tools in a library.

Eugene S. Mitchell is associate director for collection management at William Paterson College in Wayne, N.J. Before that he held several positions at the State University of New York at Buffalo. He received his BA from Canisius College and both his MLS and PhD from Rutgers University. The title of his dissertation was *Leadership Style in Academic Libraries*, a report which won the 1989 New Jersey Library Association Research Award.

Robert F. Moran, Jr., is assistant vice chancellor for academic affairs for technology and director of library services at Indiana University Northwest, Gary. He has been active in the Library Administration and Management Association of ALA. Moran is the author of articles on organizational structure and organizational behavior in *College & Research Libraries* and *The Journal of Academic Librarianship*. In 1990 he served as editor of the *Library Management and Consultants List*.

Richard H. Moul is presently an information specialist for Datalib, a mini-computer-based integrated library system from Centel Federal Systems in Reston, Va. Previously, he was a reference librarian in the R. Lee Hornbake Library at the University of Maryland at College Park. Moul received his MS in library science from the University of North Carolina at Chapel Hill in 1986.

Carol J. Mueller is central technical services human resources development librarian at the University of Wisconsin–Madison General Library System responsible for development, coordination and administration of a training program in the areas of NOTIS, OCLC and the technical services functions of acquisitions, cataloging and catalog editing. She holds an MLS from the University of Wisconsin–Madison School of Library and Information Studies. She is currently enrolled in the University of Wisconsin–Madison School of Business Outreach Program in Total Quality Management.

Hannelore B. Rader is director of the Cleveland State University Library. She has been active in the American Library Association and served as president of the Association of College and Research Libraries, chair of numerous committees and on the Council of ALA. She has spoken on and published articles regarding user instruction and library organization and management.

Donald E. Riggs is dean of the University Library and professor of information and library studies at the University of Michigan, Ann Arbor. In addition to serving as an academic library dean/director, he has been a school librarian, a public library trustee, and consultant for all types of libraries. He is the author or editor of five other books and 42 journal articles and technical reports. In 1991 he was the recipient of the Hugh Atkinson Memorial Award for his innovation and risk-taking in library technology.

Susan Stewart is the life and health sciences librarian at the University of Nevada, Reno. She received her BA at the University of Nevada, Reno, and her MLS at the University of Denver. She has been active in both the Nevada and the American Library associations. Her publications include articles in *Science & Technology Libraries*, *Microform Review* and one in progress for *Reference Services Review*.

Dianne Hamby Wright received a BS degree in education from Valdosta State College and an MS degree in library science from Florida State University. She has done additional graduate work toward the MBA. She is employed by Odum Library, Valdosta State College, where she is an associate professor of library science and has held various positions, most recently head of reference. Her professional interests include reference service, online searching, bibliographic instruction, and union lists.

Gisela M. Webb is assistant to the dean of libraries at Arizona State University in Tempe. She holds an MLS from Vanderbilt University. She has written numerous articles on personnel and library management issues and is the co-author, with Jennifer Cargill, of *Managing Libraries in Transition* and editor of *Human Resources Management in Libraries*. Webb is currently pursuing a doctorate in public administration at Arizona State University.